Joseph A. Strapac

Southern Pacific Review

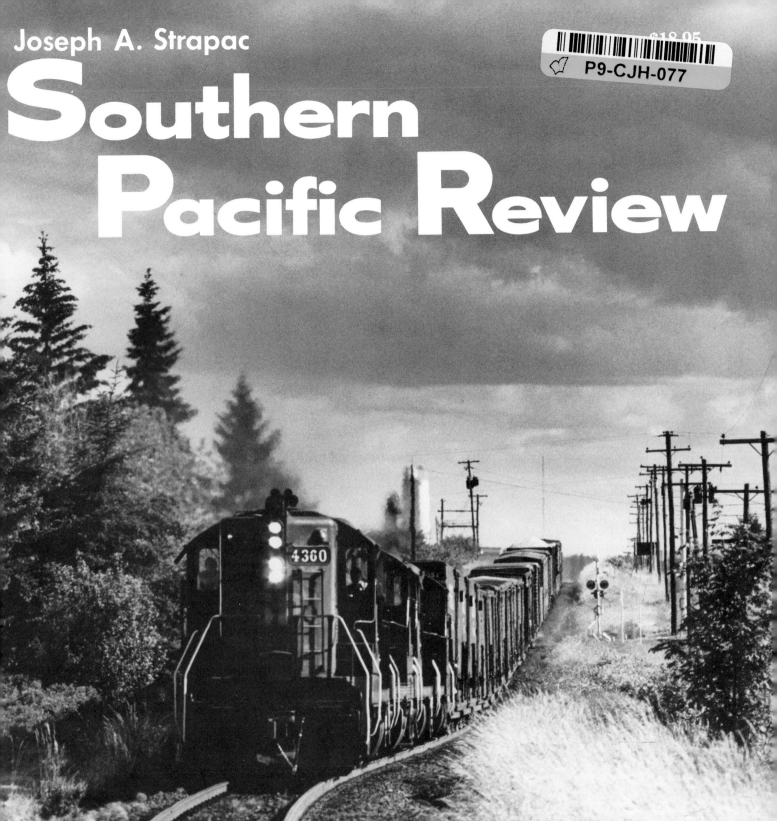

Published by the

Pacific Coast Chapter
of the Railway & Locomotive
Historical Society

Design, Layout, and Production by

Shade Tree Books
Post Office Box 2268
Huntington Beach, CA 92647

—February, 1986—

ISBN 0-930742-13-3

David P. *who* wants a cab ride? *(Kyle Brehm)*

ACKNOWLEDGEMENTS

Our front cover photo this year depicts the ultimate in SP Baldwins, one of four AS-616 units fitted with virtually every accessory the builder and the railroad could imagine. "Black Widow" #5275 was photographed by John E. Shaw at Mission Junction, across the Los Angeles River from Union Station. The date is December of 1954; few roadswitchers had as yet been repainted from traditional tiger stripes.

The rear cover illustrates a generation's difference in C-C diesels, as well as the new wave in paint schemes. At the top is a photo by Kenneth L. Douglas of Baldwin AS-616 #5231 in tiger stripes on May 1, 1954. The location is Randolph and Alameda Streets, south of downtown Los Angeles on the San Pedro Branch—in the days when Baldwin roadswitchers were in charge of this important line. Below appears newly-rebuilt SD45 #7551 as it emerged from the Sacramento Shops August 9, 1985, in a photo by Richard H. Denison of the California State Railroad Museum. Both Santa Fe and Southern Pacific released premerger- painted SD45 units early in August, to the intense interest of the enthusiast community. Those large letters on the hood are offset to make room for an additional "SF" once

the merger has been approved and implemented.

The title page picture is from the camera of Dick Dorn, illustrating the westbound *Northsider* on July 1, 1976 on the West Side Branch north of Corvallis, Oregon. Four SD9 "Cadillacs" are on the point: #4360, 4359, 3907, and 3914.

We're proud to point out that this book presents the work of no less than eighty-five different photographers or collectors. No one person can photographically "capture" a railroad the size and scope of the SP; that is why we encourage black-and-white photographic contributions. Payment is in the form of a complimentary book upon publication. We'd like to hear from you!

The six editions so far of this book have been supported financially by the Pacific Coast Chapter of the Railway and Locomotive Historical Society, whose officers and directors have continued their encouragement since 1976. A special note of thanks goes to former Chapter Chairman Brian Thompson for suggesting this project in the beginning. Directors Fred Stindt and Stuart Forsythe, both former chairmen themselves, have provided ongoing backing for an effort which they rarely see until after bindery work is completed.

International Standard Book Number

0-930742-13-3

Southern Pacific's Baldwin Diesels

The darkest days of World War II didn't prevent Baldwin's photographer from lining up five new VO-1000 switchers for a classic group portrait. Interesting details abound in this photograph taken on February 27, 1942— including the cast-steel frame and pilot beam and a buffer shank cast as part of the coupler.
(H. L. Broadbelt collection)

Southern Pacific intended to begin buying diesel switchers in the spring of 1938, and even renumbered its small 0-8-0 squadron to make room in the 1300 series for them. Just what locomotive designs SP had in mind has been lost to history, but a safe bet would include a few Wintons and a few Alco high-hoods; as of this date, Baldwin had not issued a diesel catalogue.

A business downturn in 1937-38 postponed SP's initial purchases of diesel switchers until the spring of 1939. Even then, only one locomotive builder, Electro-Motive, was offering a catalogue of mass-produced diesel units for all services. EMC had invested heavily in a new locomotive factory and was agressively pushing its new standardized switchers; the builder would gladly send a demonstrator diesel to any railroad that wanted to try one. In April of 1939, SP placed an EMC SW-1 demonstrator in service at Oakland, immediately buying it after tests. This 600- horsepower machine was an ordinary production-line switcher, essentially identical to every other SW-1 built between 1939 and 1950.

Even in 1940, Baldwin wasn't really "in production" with diesels; eight per month was the most that were turned out of Eddystone any time during the year. In fact, it wasn't until July and August of 1941 that Baldwin's diesel production line swung into action, at a rate of ten units per month. Baldwin was clearly late to the party.

It can be argued that Baldwin's management was inordinately hesitant to invest the millions of dollars necessary to develop a competitive locomotive early enough in the diesel's evolution. Even after the production limitations of World War II were lifted, Baldwin wasn't ready with modern road locomotives until 1950. By then, potential buyers had already established their product loyalties with Electro-Motive or Alco.

Southern Pacific was to purchase only 192 diesel units from Baldwin between 1941 and 1953, but this total was still greater than that of any other Western railroad. SP bought nothing but Baldwin and B-L-H roadswitchers until 1952 and continued to buy B-L-H switchers until 1953. Long after neighboring roads had abandoned Baldwin products, Southern Pacific remained convinced of their usefulness.

Although Southern Pacific never tried to "preserve" particular brands of diesel locomotives, thirty-nine B-L-H switchers were still in use on the SP as late as 1973-74. A testimonial is present in that fact.

SOUTHERN PACIFIC'S BALDWIN DIESELS
DELIVERIES, 1941 — 1953

MODEL	SP CLASS	BUILT	ORIGINAL NOS.	1965 NOS.	QUANTITY	
B-B SWITCHERS						
VO-660	DS-7	1941	1021-1022	——	2	
						2
VO-1000	DS-102	1941	1320-1324	——	5	
	DS-103	1942	1325-1329	——	5	
	DS-106	1943	1375-1376	1856-1857	2	
	DS-107	1943	1377-1378	——	2	
		1944	1371-1374	1858-1859	4	
		1944	1379-1385	1860-1862	7	
						25
DS-4-4-1000	DS-108	1948	1393-1402	1863-1869	10	
						10
S-12	DS-110	1951	1442-1463	2100-2120	22	
	DS-112	1952	105-107	2121-2123	3	
	DS-114	1952-53	1492-1513	2124-2145	22	
	DS-118	1953	1539-1550	2146-2157	12	
						59
A1A-A1A ROADSWITCHERS						
DRS-6-4-15	DF-100	1948	5200-5202	——	2	
						2
C-C ROADSWITCHERS AND CABLESS UNITS						
DRS-6-6-15	DF-101	1949	5203-5212	——	10	
		1949	187-188	——	2	
	DF-102	1949	189-190	——	2	
	DF-103	1949	5213-5217	——	5	
	DF-104	1950	5218-5226	——	9	
						28
DRS-6-6-15B	DF-105	1950	5227 (5500;4900)	——	1	
						1
AS-616	DF-106	1950	5228-5239	——	12	
	DF-107	1951	5240-5248	——	9	
	DF-108	1951	5249	——	1	
	DF-109	1951	5250-5252	——	3	
	DF-112	1952	5253-5278	——	26	
	DF-113	1952	177-184	——	8	
						59
AS-616B	DF-110	1951	5501-5502	——	2	
	DF-111	1951	5503-5505	——	3	
						5
					Total:	**192**

Prewar VO-660's

After obtaining seven EMC SW-1's and three Alco HH-660's in its 1939 switcher program, SP asked for fifteen units from three builders to be delivered in the spring of 1941: eight SW-1 units, five of Alco's new S-1 model, and two Baldwin VO-660's (one each of the Alco and EMC units were for the T&NO).

Baldwins #1021-1022 were shipped on March 29 and placed in service at El Paso on April 15. For the record, these VO-660s were the fifteenth and sixteenth of their model to be manufactured by Baldwin. They carried inline six-cylinder VO engines #1713 and 1711, part of a batch ordered for future production the previous July 5.

All prewar Southern Pacific switchers were painted in SP's version of EMD switcher demonstrator colors of black with horizontal aluminum stripes along the hood and running board. Lettering was "Southern Pacific Lines" until 1946.

The VO-660 units were immediately moved to the Bay Area for service and were at work there by early May. In 1943 and 1944, it was decided to concentrate Baldwin and Electro-Motive units at Los Angeles and keep the Alcos in the Bay Area; thenceforth, Baldwins were rarities in Oakland.

Pictures on the following page illustrate some of the development of the VO-660; even though SP purchased only two, they were kept up-to-date with more recent Baldwin production by retrofits of new equipment as their builder refined the design. Most apparent is the exhaust, which began as a short, single stack ahead of the cab, which carried a horizontal muffler inside the hood. Unfortunately, exhaust plumbing was located over the main generator and close enough to the engine air intakes that it radiated excess heat on both. Experimenting at the factory yielded two optional answers: two stacks or four—as illustrated, SP had an example of each.

As built, the VO-660's (and early VO-1000's) carried a 100-gallon radiator expansion tank inside the hood under the headlight; this capacity was found to be inadequate, and Baldwin supplied parts to add 200 additional gallons of coolant capacity atop the hood right behind the headlight. By the end of the War, all SP Baldwin switchers carried this feature.

Finally, there was a small problem with radiator air flow. As delivered, the VO-660s drew in cooling air from the nose and blew it out through the hood roof behind the headlight. A fine mesh grille on the top tended to block airflow, so side ports were needed as well. When the builder adopted a more open roof grille (that incidentally could support a man), the side ports became redundant and were blocked off.

In April of 1948, both VO-660's were leased by the Pacific Electric; they were soon relettered and fitted with trolley poles to actuate grade crossing signals. The PE at that time carried more freight in California than either Western Pacific or Union Pacific, and frequently leased steam or diesel engines from SP as needed. By 1952-53, PE had converted the bulk of its electrified lines to rail signal actuation and began removing trolley poles from diesels after that date. In 1956, all the leased Baldwins were returned to SP in exchange for EMD switchers.

The next six years found the VO-660 units frequently stored or laboring in obscurity, due to their low power. Even though well-maintained, they were advancing in years; SP had little for them to do anymore. In 1962, the Los Angeles Division received permission to vacate them from the roster; they were sold for scrap to Luria Brothers at the harbor.

In later years, the two VO-660's were almost synonymous with the Pacific Electric, but they also performed close-out duties for the Interurban Electric in the Bay Area. Less than a month after entering service, #1021 is moving cuts of ten motor cars from the abandoned West Alameda shops on May 12, 1941 to storage at West Oakland. Some of these cars would eventually serve with #1021 in Southern California. *(J. C. Hammond)*

Evolution of the VO-660's

VO-660 EVOLUTION: In its factory portrait on March 29, 1941, #1021 featured a single short stack, "Southern Pacific Lines" lettering, no radiator expansion tank, an open side radiator grille, and no armrests or awnings. Wheels were striped for the picture; the cast steps show up well in this low light.
(H. L. Broadbelt collection)

AT AGE THREE: Still in original paint and lettering at Vernon and Alameda Streets in Los Angeles on February 27, 1944, #1022 has already received significant mechanical modifications. Most importantly, it now carries four exhaust stacks—allowing the engine and generator to run much cooler. It also has a small radiator expansion tank behind the headlight. A typical wartime light-dispersion shield covers the headlight.
(Gerald M. Best)

Evolving still at age six, #1022 poses at Alhambra on April 30, 1947. Orange tiger stripes and large lettering are obvious, but compare the still-larger expansion tank with the picture above. A walkway grille has been added atop the hood, as have two louvered doors for the airbox above the letters "FIC". Most importantly, #1022 has received a replacement engine with a latter-day two-stack exhaust manifold. Finally, the side grille has been plated over.
(William Bassler)

Milling traction enthusiasts from one of Pacific Electric's final Northern District excursions part to make way for this westbound freight extra at Oneonta Junction in South Pasadena in August of 1951. All PE freight engines used roller trolleys, and were liberally stencilled with safety slogans. The #1021 still has four exhaust stacks. *(Craig Rasmussen collection)*

West of the Los Angeles River in Long Beach, SP and PE shared a freight house on Pico Boulevard. In this 1949 photo by the late Stuart Liebman, #1021 models its neatly hand-lettered road name and mis-labeled "DES-107" class identification—which should read "DS-7". Early VO's sported this relatively flat roof contour and safety bars in the lower cab windows. *(Craig Rasmussen collection)*

Decisive evidence that neither VO-660 ever received grey paint is found in this final picture, as the pair was on its way to scrap at Long Beach Harbor on March 14, 1963 in black and solid orange colors. Over the years, both engines had been fitted with more serviceable welded steel steps to replace the original cast pieces. Vacated in November of 1962, #1021-1022 were among the very first SP diesels to leave the roster. *(Ted VanKlaveren collection)*

This anonymous VO-660, photographed at Taylor Yard in 1949, was built in March of 1942 for the Basic Magnesium Company of Henderson, Nevada. After the War it was sold to the Shea Company for construction duties on Kaiser Steel's Eagle Mountain Railroad; SP leased it in August of 1948. About 1952 it was sold to the Longview, Portland & Northern as their #1001, and nearly earned immortality in a museum before finally being cut up. *(Strapac collection)*

Prewar VO-1000's

Much more to SP's liking were the Baldwin VO-1000 units, the first five of which, #1320-1324, were delivered in July of 1941. Another five, #1320-1329, arrived in March, 1942. With eight cylinders, three feet more length, and a thousand horsepower, the VO-1000's were otherwise clones of the 660's delivered three months earlier.

Mechanical features as first delivered—and later modified—paralleled experience with the smaller units; similar retrofits took place with exhausts and radiator expansion tanks. These early units also had some difficulty with air intake, both in volume and filter efficiency, which explains the hinged, louvered panels added later high on the hood near the cab. Underneath were much larger, washable filters that drew their air supply from outside the hood, where ambient temperatures were lower.

All these 1941-42 engines were built with a

Apparently SP's first series of VO-1000's, #1320-1324, never posed for an official Baldwin photo; they left the plant in June and July of 1941. Five virtually identical machines were turned out in February of 1942. These DES-102's faithfully copied visible features of the VO-660's, except for longer hoods with more doors for access to the eight-cylinder engine. *(H. L. Broadbelt collection)*

By March of 1946 (at Bakersfield), SP had given #1321 "the works;" the combination of tiger stripes and "Lines" lettering was quite rare. It now has four stacks, expansion tank, top walkway grille, covered side grilles, and the louvered doors high on the rear of the hood for access to airbox filters. Incidentally, all the VO-1000's were apparently able to retain cast steps throughout their careers. *(Guy L. Dunscomb)*

During the forties and fifties, Pacific Electric generated more freight traffic in California than either the UP or WP, as demonstrated by this impressive drag at Sunnyslope near Rosemead Boulevard on the Monrovia- Glendora Line in July of 1951...a few months prior to abandonment of this trackage. The raised trolley pole activated crossing signals; once signal circuits were converted to rail actuation, the poles and overhead were removed. *(Craig Rasmussen collection)*

relatively shallow arch to the cab roof, with window safety bars in the lower segment of the rear cab windows. An additional hood door was needed for access to the eight-cylinder engine, but otherwise there was little visible to differentiate the two models.

Most of their service careers after the war were spent in the Los Angeles area, where they were even pressed into road helper service on occasion. The #1320-1322 were leased to the Pacific Electric in 1948, followed by #1325-1327 in 1949; the others were added to the PE roster in 1950 and 1951. As was the practice with the VO-660's, all received trolley poles and hand-lettered "Pacific Electric" identification at PE's Torrance shops. This unique lettering did not survive the full time span the VO's worked on the PE, since that road's paint shops

went out of business in 1954. The #1323 was returned to SP in April of 1954, while the others lasted until October of 1956.

At age 21, SP decided to write them off. The first to go were #1321 and 1323, which were sent for scrap, respectively, to Precision Engineering and Luria at Los Angeles Harbor. In 1963, the #1325 was scrapped by SP at Eugene, Oregon. The year 1964 saw #1320, 1322, and 1324 go in trade to General Electric for new U25B's. The remaining four were all vacated in 1965; #1329 went to Electro-Motive and #1326 was scrapped by Purdy. The #1327-1328 were traded to Alco in October of 1965...after the former had been assigned #1855 in the new numbering system. However, it went to scrap in its old number.

A perfectly-lighted picture at Los Angeles on November 9, 1947 shows DES-102 #1324 at its peak...before SP began buying Electro-Motive NW2's in quantity. That upper horizontal stripe goes right across all the louvers; only a few VO's carried a sheet-steel number plate under the headlight, but most of the early VO's were retrofitted with four stacks. *(Allan Youell)*

Lurking among the red-painted electric locomotives at Pacific Electric's Macy Street Yard (near the General Hospital), leased #1321 was photographed about 1948. The added louvered doors for the replacement air box at the top rear of the hood are prominent here; PE's trolley pole installation required addition of steel "tables" to support the pneumatic trolley bases. *(Arthur Lloyd: Hansen collection)*

Early VO #1322 was leased to the Pacific Electric on October 8, 1948, and was to become a fixture on that road, not departing until the PE decided to change over to EMD power and eliminate its remaining electric freight locomotives in one swoop in October of 1956. Already lettered for the parent road, #1322 languishes at PE's San Bernardino facilities on June 9, 1956—still fitted with redundant trolley poles.
(Robert E. Smith)

A cut of sparkling new Pacific Fruit Express ice refrigerator cars is followed by one of SP's old "Harriman" coaches, downgraded to serve as a transfer caboose. The overhead at Macy Street is gone now, dating this picture about 1953, but PE #1326 still carries trolley poles. By 1956, PE will be virtually dieselized, with most of its long-term Baldwins given back to parent SP. *(Ken Douglas)*

Halloween colors and non-standard "stacked" lettering distinguish DS-103 #1329 at Glendale on a caboose hop on May 29, 1964. Late in their careers, the VO's received a small semicircular cutout in their frame side rails to better clear their fuel fillers. The "outhouse on a shingle" transfer cabooses are described in more detail in our 1981 REVIEW. *(Ken Douglas)*

Two of the 1941-42 VO-1000's, #1320 and 1328, were given new replacement engines, apparently on warranty, about 1945. Since these engines were built to a later Baldwin specification, they carried different exhaust manifolds; as a result, they sported this distinctive two-stack treatment illustrated by #1328 at Alhambra station on January 9, 1949. In April of 1950, #1328 would be leased to the Pacific Electric for a six-year term. *(William Bassler)*

A two-stack VO-1000, viewed from above, illustrates many features not apparent at ground level. Especially significant is the complex cast frame, neatly scalloped on each corner for steps. The front of the hood top clearly illustrates both radiator expansion tank and the reinforced grille over the radiator outlet. In August of 1964, #1320 had but days left before retirement. *(David C. Lustig)*

11

The Wartime VO-1000's

Everyone has candidates for the title of "ugliest locomotive;" how about a vote for "best-looking switcher?" In Philadelphia snow on January 30, 1943, DES-106 #1375 displays the inherent grace of good design. Although the factory has now installed a full radiator expansion tank, side radiator grilles are still apparent (and will be until September of 1943 with #1378). The cab roof has more curvature by this time.
(H. L. Broadbelt collection)

Strapped for switchers during World War II, SP would have liked to have more of anything. As it turned out, during 1943-45, the War Production Board grudgingly let SP/T&NO have 40 Alco S-2's and a paltry fifteen Baldwin VO-1000's. In 1943 and 1944, #1371- 1385 were delivered in this order: #1375-1378 (1943), #1379-1382 (1944), #1371-1374 (1944), and #1383-1385 (1944). It took seventeen months for all to arrive!

Components were similar to those aboard #1320-29, but most of the "fixes" described above were incorporated during production; even the single stack was made to run cooler. The cast frame (with integral steps) was seven inches longer, and in May of 1944 was modified to eliminate the graceful curves around the cab and step gussets. The last five units, #1373-74 and #1383-85, were delivered

after this running change and thus had angled frame corners.

At least seven were leased to the PE; most received both lettering and trolley poles during their stay: #1371, 73, 74, 77-79, 81. PE returned its Baldwins in 1956. In May of 1962, #1371, 1384, and 1385 were all vacated, followed by #1379 and #1383 in 1963. The #1374 and 1378 were dropped in 1964, while #1372 and 1377 lasted until 1965. The #1372 went to scrap in October of 1965 with its old number, but had been assigned the "ghost" number 1858. The remaining units became #1856-57 and #1859-62. In 1966, #1860-62 were vacated, followed in 1967 by #1857 and 1859. The #1856, built in 1943 as the first of the group, was last to go; they were sold to EMD in July of 1969.

Baldwin VO's built after May of 1944 dispensed with the curved sheetmetal trim around the battery boxes seen in the picture above; a few months after that, SP adopted "tiger stripe" paint for additional visibility. In consequence, late VO's arrived looking very different, even though still lettered "Southern Pacific Lines." DES-107 #1385, placed in service in July of 1944, has stopped for the Company photographer at Los Angeles in early 1945 to show off an early application of train radio.
(James H. Harrison collection)

This VO-1000, built in June of 1944, doesn't have the side radiator grille intakes seen on earlier examples; it also carries a short single stack, in contrast to #1375 opposite, which has no visible stack extension at all. Stack extensions were found to be useful; in 1945, Baldwin would go over to dual stacks, but by then SP wasn't ordering VO's. At Los Angeles, November 24, 1946. *(Allan Youell)*

By the late forties, all the VO's had been gathered in Los Angeles. In gleaming tiger stripes at Taylor Yard on January 16, 1949, #1371 displays its aluminum-painted radio equipment box on the hood just ahead of the cab. This March, 1944 Eddystone alumnus was one of the last to receive curved side trim. *(Allan Youell)*

VO's #1371-1385 weren't delivered in numerical order; #1378 was shipped a full twelve months previous to #1374 above—in May of 1943—and thus appears with curved side trim. In a photo taken about 1954, #1378 is very obviously hand-lettered for Pacific Electric, although no trolley poles were ever installed, since it was leased only between 1952 and 1956. This was the only VO known to carry a three-chime horn. *(Victor Rawstron)*

Very late in the VO era, #1381 pokes its nose into bay #8 at Taylor Yard's diesel shop in Los Angeles. The date is November 22, 1964, and within a year this unit will become #1861; it won't be retired until March of 1966. By this time all stencilled class designations had disappeared from cab sides. Compared to the 1320's, these late VO's had taller cab doors and more cab headroom. *(David C. Lustig)*

Freshly painted in Espee's ill-advised "halloween" orange-and-black colors, 1943-vintage VO #1375 gleams on the paint track at Taylor roundhouse in Los Angeles in June of 1958. Only applied to a few dozen diesel units, this somber color scheme was quickly superceded by grey and scarlet in the fall of 1958. The #1375 would endure to become #1856, the very last VO to serve.

(Ray Whitaker collection)

Still carrying the supposedly fragile cast steps it came with in January of 1943, VO #1856 (#1375) was captured by the author's camera at the Links Yard near Chinatown in Los Angeles on a very late August 19, 1967. It was the first of the #1371-1385 wartime VO's to be delivered, and the last to be retired—serving twenty-six years. Since its picture above as #1375, the frame side has been cut away to make room for a fuel filler.

Postwar "S-10" Switchers

Beginning in 1948, Baldwin abandoned the eight-cylinder VO engine, replacing it with a dimensionally-similar turbocharged inline six, called a 606-C. Among other benefits of the new prime mover were increased reliability and the inherent ability of a turbocharged diesel to generate more horsepower without wasting fuel. The turbocharger utilized heat energy in the exhaust gases (that was formerly wasted) to drive a turbine that compressed intake air, increasing the weight of the intake charge; more horsepower resulted. Two visible features of the turbocharged "S-10" were a small bulge on the fireman's side of the hood underneath the stack and the stack itself, which was now conical in shape.

Southern Pacific, planning its first postwar switcher order for the Pacific Lines (T&NO was buying Alco S-2's in 1947), chose the new Baldwin design. Ten of them (clumsily labelled "DS-4-4-1000" by their builder but known simply as "S-10" by the SP) were ordered for delivery in September of 1948. Their numbers were to be SP #1393-1399 and Pacific Electric #1660-1662; the latter three to be fitted with trolley poles at the factory. Unfortunately for later diesel enthusiasts, SP had a change of heart soon after placing the order, scrubbing plans for PE switchers. Instead, the last three became SP #1400-1402. All were delivered in orange stripes with large "Southern Pacific" lettering on the hoods.

Southern Pacific's Texas & New Orleans subsidiary leased four S-10s for an extended evaluation; #1393-1394 and #1401-1402 were delivered new to the T&NO at Humble, Texas. They worked for the T&NO in Pacific Lines numbers until April of 1949, when they were sent west. They were not well-received, and as a result the T&NO didn't order any Baldwin switchers until 1951-52.

All ten S-10s soon went to work in Los Angeles, where they were to remain throughout their careers. The author has no record of any of them being leased to the Pacific Electric, although assuredly some did serve that subsidiary briefly. As the years passed, most of them were moved to new assignments in Oregon; by mid-1967 only #1863-1865 remained in Los Angeles— but #1863 and 1865 were transferred north in 1971.

Relatively little modification was performed on these units during the fifteen to twenty-four years they served on the SP. After 1958, many were repainted in solid orange and black "halloween" colors, and most finally received grey and scarlet paint. One or two were fitted with rotary cab-roof beacons, and all had their frame edges cut away for fuel-filler clearance.

Three were vacated prior to the 1965 renumbering. The #1398 was sold to Precision Engineering in November of 1963 as a GE trade, while #1395 met the same fate eleven months later. The #1394 was traded to EMD for an SW-1200 in December of 1964. On the eve of the renumbering, #1399 had to be written off, after being assigned new #1866; the others became #1863-1865 and #1867-1869. The #1868 was wrecked in 1966 (a photo appears on page 17), while #1864 and 1867 went to EMD in 1969. The last three were #1863, 1865, and 1869, which all lasted until 1972, when they were traded to EMD.

Espee's first postwar Baldwin switchers (ten DS-4-4-1000's) arrived in September of 1948, after the builder had converted to six-cylinder turbocharged engines with single, fat stacks. Overall length has been reduced, and the cast frame has bolt-on steps. The builder's plate, above the front wheel, is now five-sided and says "Baldwin-Westinghouse." #1393 is stencilled "DES-107," but should read "DES-108!"
(H. L. Broadbelt collection)

The ten "S-10" switchers in class DS-108 were fixtures around Southern California for years. At the Safeway warehouse at Vernon and Alameda in Los Angeles on July 29, 1957, #1397 sports a freshly re-painted cab marked "radio equipped" and a rare rotary beacon on the roof. Installation of the tur-bocharged engine caused the builder to add a small hood bulge under the letters "CIF." *(Ken Douglas)*

In the renumbering of 1965, the seven remaining DS-4-4-1000's in the series #1393-1402 became #1863-1869 (three had been retired previously). Grey paint and a semicircular fuel filler cutout mark #1864—the former #1396—at Firestone Park in South Los Angeles on June 3, 1967. By this time, the side number windows were painted over. *(Joseph A. Strapac)*

The last three DS-4-4-1000's, #1863, 1865 and 1869, remained on active duty until the early months of 1972. Here's a begrimed, halloween-painted #1869 (old #1402) at rest in Portland on October 14, 1968. By now, both the number window and over-hood cab windows have been covered with sheet steel. *(Larry Russell:Douglas collection)*

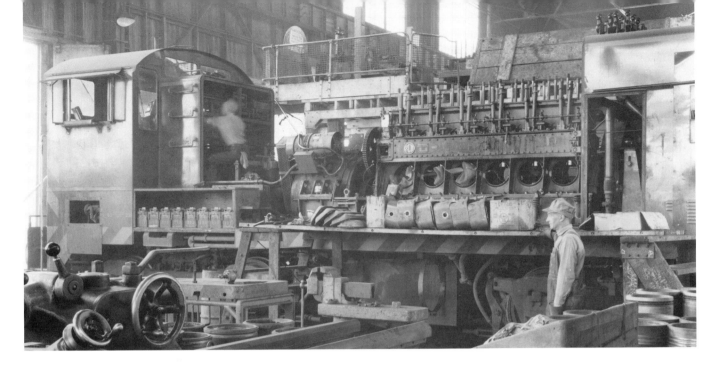

Inside Taylor Shop for a serious overhaul in 1952, hoodless #1400 explains its internal arrangements. The six-cylinder engine sits rather far forward, but is missing its turbosupercharger—normally located above the traction generator. Note the eight batteries ahead of the cab. It will be a while before #1400 is back out on the road.

(Richard Steinheimer)

We couldn't resist this very late view of #1865 (#1397) at the Portland roundhouse on February 21, 1972. The 1000-hp. Baldwin is only four months away from retirement, but carries an ACI light-bar sticker on its hood. More unusual, though, is relocation of the chime horns down from the cab roof. It's possible that the entire center hood section was transferred from another Baldwin, explaining that odd lettering.

(Frank Guernsey:Towler collection)

In late 1966, thousand-horsepower #1868 was wrecked in a switching accident in Los Angeles. Before shipping it off to Luria Brothers at the Harbor for scrap, Taylor Yard shop forces put the hulk on shop trucks and removed all parts that would be useful in keeping other Baldwins running. Even the fuel and air tanks had been removed by February 11, 1967.

(Bryan Griebenow)

17

The S-12 Switchers

Espee's largest single order for Baldwin diesel switchers was placed in 1950, when order #P-199 was entered with Baldwin for twenty-two new model S-12 units, class DS-110, numbered 1442 through 1463, for shipment between January and April of 1951.

After November 30, 1950, Baldwin became the Baldwin-Lima-Hamilton Corporation; technically all S-12's in the #1442-1463 series were products of B-L-H. However, the new corporate logo didn't appear on builder's plates until the following March. As it turned out, the first SP diesels delivered with new B-L-H plates were #1456 and 5248, both shipped in March. The new plate was rectangular and bore stamped numerals, rather than cast.

The DS-110 locomotives were delivered all over the Pacific Lines between January 23 and April 24, 1951. Two modifications made to most DS-110 units were addition of train number indicators ahead of the cab atop the hood and train radio equipment. With a narrower frame edge than their predecessors, these S-12's did not need a fuel-filler clearance cutout.

During the sixties, most of the Los Angeles-assigned DS-110 units moved to Northern California or Oregon; by the renumbering in 1965, all of them had departed from Southern California. Only #1447 didn't survive to be renumbered—it was sold for scrap to Purdy in Oakland in November of 1963. Remaining units became #2100-2120 in October, 1965, and were reclassified BS412-1.

The #2108 was vacated in March of 1966, very soon after receiving its new number. The next retired was #2105, sold to EMD in March of 1970 and scrapped for them at Associated Metals in Benicia. The year 1971 saw departure of #2118 and

S-12's #1442-1463 arrived early in 1951; many of them found immediate homes in the Los Angeles area. Out on the road in bucolic Santa Fe Springs in July of 1957, #1450 has a local freight in tow. By now, Baldwin was installing dual sealed-beam headlights on switchers; from #1456 up, builders' plates would read "Baldwin-Lima-Hamilton." *(Ken Douglas)*

In their early years, the twenty-two S-12's in class DS-110 were scattered systemwide; this Company photo was taken in Central California about 1953. Most of this class had their train number indicators installed back near the cab on the hood. Bolt-on steps and pilot beam are prominent here, even though the frame itself is still a casting. *(James H. Harrison collection)*

At Ashland, Oregon, on September 26, 1956, S-12 #1462 backs a cut down a lead. The air tanks are already painted black, and this engine has a rectangular Baldwin-Lima-Hamilton plate on the frame side. The #1462 was set up for service at Ashland on May 19, 1951; more than five years later it was still working there, without train number indicators. *(R. W. Biermann:Douglas collection)*

After the renumbering of 1965, DS-110's #1442-1463 became #2100-2120; only #1447 wasn't around to be changed. Onetime #1457, now #2114, still carried black and orange paint at Portland on December 7, 1968. The glass engine number window high on the hood is still there, but painted over. *(Bryan Griebenow collection)*

Chime-horn-equipped #2104, originally #1446, was a longtime regular at the small yard in the far northern California logging town of Weed. One of relatively few DS-110's to receive grey paint, it sports Automatic Car Identification color bars and chime horns in this 1969 view. The glass engine number window has been plated over with sheet steel. *(Henry Brueckman:Griebenow collection)*

The most camera-shy of all SP's Baldwin diesels were the T&NO class DS-112 S-12's, #105-107. They were built in February of 1952 and generally ignored by railfan photographers, despite their significance as the first B-L-H switchers for SP built with welded frames. Even though scheduled to be renumbered #2123 in the fall of 1965, #107 still wore its old number and tiger stripes at Houston's Englewood Yard on May 8, 1966.
(Harvey George)

As late as December of 1968, #2121 was still wearing its orange stripes, displayed here at Houston. In addition to their builders' important production change to welded frames in January of 1952, these carried a small grate opening in the front of the radiator. Note also the rotating beacon and extended stack, features not common on Pacific Lines Baldwins.
(Jim Zwernemann:Griebenow collection)

Off-duty amid diesels leased from other local roads at the Port Terminal Railroad Association enginehouse in Houston in February of 1969, grey #2122 is also fitted with extended stack and rotating beacon. Both #2121 and 2122 were transferred to Los Angeles in 1970, but #2123 (old T&NO #107) was traded to Electro-Motive in April of 1967.
(Jim Hickey)

2119, while #2107 was the only vacate in 1972 (it was resold to Bethlehem Steel #11 in Vernon late that year). Ten units were written off in 1973, however, including #2106, which had collided with #2135 at Eugene in July of 1972. The last six units were sold in two batches in 1974: #2103, 13, 14, and 20 on February 19, and #2101 and 2111 that May 13. Most of them ended up being scrapped by Purdy at Chehalis, Washington.

A second group of B-L-H model S-12 switchers was the small class of three purchased by the Texas & New Orleans in January of 1952. T&NO #105-107 were class DS-112 and were the only B-L-H or Baldwin switchers bought new by the T&NO. B-L-H

had by this time abandoned the cast frame and was welding up a much thicker-appearing underbody. As a result, it was again necessary later to cut out a semicircle for fuel-filler clearance. A small louvered door was added in the front radiator area, but otherwise these units were reasonable copies of the Pacific Lines' DS-110 class delivered a year previously.

The T&NO saw no need for train number indicators, but did extend the exhaust stacks. In 1961, the T&NO was merged into the SP; in 1965, SP, Cotton Belt, and T&NO diesels were all placed in one number series; all three former T&NO DS-112s were renumbered in 1965 to #2121-2123,

Two Pacific Lines class DS-114 S-12's were transferred to the Texas & New Orleans in March of 1956. SP #1498 and 1505 became T&NO #121-122, later renumbered as #2124-2125, and transferred back to Los Angeles in 1970. Before that, in 1967, #2124 works the dock area at the Houston Ship Channel. Of all the T&NO's diesel switchers, only these two carried signal lights, which were quickly removed! *(Ray Kenley)*

but the #2123 was traded to Electro-Motive in April of 1967. The other two were transferred to Los Angeles early in late 1969, where they worked only briefly before being sold to Chrome Crankshaft, a local locomotive dealer. Amador Central, a shortline in the Sierra foothills, bought #2121 for further service in June of 1972, while Chrome cut up #2122 for parts in 1973.

On April 4, 1952, Southern Pacific placed an order for 22 new S-12s at $107,575 apiece. The new units, #1492-1513, were placed in service between November of 1952 and March of 1953 as class DS-114. Although mechanically identical to T&NO's DS-112's, the Pacific Lines units were fitted with Mars signal lights beside their headlights in large housings. As before, they entered service at diverse locations; in their early years they were found all over the Pacific Lines. Most received train number indicators and had the original "fish horn" moved from behind the stack to the cab roof.

In 1956, two DS-114 units were "sold" to the T&NO to replace two Fairbanks-Morse switchers originally intended to go there. SP decided to keep all the F-M's together, and sent #1498 and 1505 to become T&NO #121-122.

After the renumbering, the T&NO duo became #2124- 2125, while the twenty on the Pacific Lines filled #2126-2145. Along with the ex-T&NO DS-112s, #2124-2125 were moved to Los Angeles in November, 1969. SP promptly sold #2124 to Chrome Crankshaft, who resold it to Ketchikan Pulp in Alaska, but #2125 was overhauled and re-

painted and joined L. A.'s local B-L-H switcher fleet. Most of the other DS-114s not already in Oregon were sent there in the sixties; only #2143 worked out its days in Southern California. The #2124, 2127, and 2143 were all vacated in 1970; the rest of the DS-114 fleet was decimated between 1972 and 1974, however, when the entire class was sent to dealers for scrap or resale. In May of 1974, #2138 became the last DS-114 to leave the roster, when it was sold to Purdy at Chehalis, Washington.

Finally, in 1953, SP ordered its last Baldwins; twelve S-12s to be delivered that October and November. They were class DS-118, #1539-1550, and were equipped with Mars signal lights, multiple-unit controls (SP's only Baldwin switchers with m.u.), and outside handrails. Other spotting features included a small oval-section stack and cast equipment-trust plates attached to the side sills. The extra options added 7100 pounds to their weight; they cost $108,676 each. As usual, they were painted in "tiger stripe" orange and black colors. A few were redone in solid orange in the late fifties, but all of them eventually received grey and scarlet paint. The renumbering of 1965 placed them in the #2146-2157 series.

More than any other Baldwins, the DS-118s were almost exclusively found near Los Angeles—from delivery until retirement between 1970 and 1974. Only three were ever formally reassigned to Oregon: #2149, 2153, and 2156, and they were not moved north until the middle of 1970. (The #2149 and 2156 had been leased in 1970 to the California Western to

Backing across the eastbound Sunset Route from Los Angeles Union Passenger Terminal, #1499 is pushing, cab first, while #1500 pulls on the other end. Twenty-two of these DS-114's, #1492-1513, were delivered between October of 1952 and February of 1953. All were fitted with unique side-by-side signal lights and the small radiator grate first seen on T&NO #105-107. At Mission Junction, Los Angeles, April 27, 1957. *(Ken Douglas)*

In almost mint condition, #1506 awaits its next call in the afternoon sun at Sparks, Nevada on May 7, 1954. The train number indicator and classification lights were added after delivery. The #1506 went to work on January 4, 1953; in 1965 it was to become #2138. It wasn't retired until 1974.

(Ray Whitaker collection)

...And where were *you* on November 22, 1963? The author, then a student at Long Beach State College, was at the Harbor Belt Line enginehouse in Wilmington (Los Angeles Harbor) photographing orange and black DS-114 #1511, at that time on lease to the joint operating agency which provided neutral switching at the harbor for all four line-haul roads.

Seven days after the picture opposite of #1511, a young Joe McMillan photographed T&NO #122 at his hometown of Yorktown, Texas. Formerly SP #1505, T&NO #122 has already had its signal light plated over, but the T&NO has added a "firecracker" radio antenna and a small number plate under the headlights. In two years, it will become #2125.

replace some CW units lost in a wreck; when their tenure there was complete, they were sent to Eugene.)

Disposal began in 1970, when #2155 was dispatched to Associated Metals as an EMD trade. Two more, #2147 and 2151, were cut up in 1972 by National Metals. In 1973, Purdy scrapped #2149 and 2153 at Chehalis, #2146 and 2148 were sold to

California Western, and #2152 went to Chrome Crankshaft for resale. In August of 1974, the end finally came for SP's Baldwins, when #2150, 2154, and #2157 were sold to Chrome Crankshaft. A decade later, all three were still working for industrial users, but the era of Baldwin diesels on the Southern Pacific was over.

A gleaming, freshly-painted #2126 takes a spin on the Klamath Falls turntable on July 29, 1969. The first of the DS-114 class, once #1492, this particular engine entered service on November 19, 1952, and was to remain on duty in Oregon until late 1973, one of the last of its class.   *(Ken Douglas)*

The ultimate in SP S-12's was class DS-118, #1539-1550, built in September and October of 1953 at a cost of $108,676 each. These were the only Baldwin switchers with multiple-unit connections and gangways, and the only ones to sport outside handrails. Another spotting feature was the oval exhaust stack. Third of the series, #1541 poses at Eddystone for an official portrait on September 29, 1953.

(H. L. Broadbelt collection)

A cab-end view of #1540 at Norwalk, California, on June 25, 1963 helps explain just how complex these final S-12's really were. With pneumatic m.u. and gangways and dual lights, platform ends got quite crowded! Fairbanks-Morse switchers #1529-1538 of May 1953 were similarly equipped. On this order only, the fuel fill has been moved to the rear of the tank. A battery recharging socket appears below "15" on the cab.

(Bryan Griebenow)

Four days after this picture (at the longtime tie-up point of Firestone Park), DS-118 #1545 was to become #2152 in the general renumbering of October, 1965, but on October 17th, that was all in the future. Significantly, the battery charging receptacle has been plated over, but #1545 still has its little illuminated number window.

(Joseph A. Strapac)

The very last Baldwin to hold a place on the Southern Pacific roster was #2157 (#1550), shipped from Eddystone on October 31, 1953. It was placed in service that November 14th, working most of its years in and around Los Angeles. The end came for the last two B-L-H units, #2150 and 2157, in August of 1974. Twenty-six months before that, #2157 was photographed in a common haunt, Links Yard in Los Angeles.
(Charles H. Cox)

Amador Central #10, westbound near Ranlett, below Martell in California's Sierra foothills, is the former Southern Pacific #2121, originally T&NO #105. It was sold by SP in August of 1970 to dealer Chrome Crankshaft, who in turn sold it in June of 1972 to the AC. The S-12 still retains the T&NO's extended stack, but now carries a "gumball" flasher on the cab roof. Six carloads of wood chips rumble downgrade on March 20, 1978.
(Don Bain)

Flash...SP Baldwins to run on PCC trucks! Or so it would appear from this picture, at Los Angeles on November 11, 1966, while a freshly-painted #2146 (formerly #1539) waited on shop trucks for its own trucks to be released from repairs. Parked next to ex-T&NO F7 #354, the S-12 has had its number window painted over; it will work until 1973, when sold to the California Western as a parts source.

(Joseph A. Strapac)

As detail-packed a picture as anyone could want, this view from the overhead footbridge at Taylor Yard on January 29, 1971 illustrates the caboose track and part of the wrecking outfit, with diner #MW7118 on the right. More prominent, however, is a former T&NO S-12 with numerous official and unofficial modifications, including chime horns, plated-over signal light, and supplemental cardboard "radiator shutters."

(David C. Lustig)

S-12 Graduates

One early graduate—that didn't travel far—was #2107, sold to Chrome Crankshaft in 1973. In turn, it became Bethlehem Steel #11 at Vernon, California, and is shown here in 1977 out on former Pacific Electric trackage behind the plant in its yellow-and-red colors. Footboards are gone, and a gumball flasher has been added.
(Jerry T. Moyers)

Chrome Crankshaft #32-31 are on their way to Geneva, Utah, where they will become United States Steel #40-41 in February of 1973. These are in actuality Southern Pacific #2132 and 2133, with temporary numbers applied over their primer paint for shipping convenience. Their new owner—a Baldwin holdout—will paint them in yellow.
(Henry Brueckman)

S-12 #2128 was traded to General Electric in November of 1972, ending up in the hands of dealer Chrome Crankshaft. It was soon sold to Koppel Bulk Terminals of Long Beach, who have a large grain elevator at dockside. Later, Koppel was acquired by AGREX, Inc., who repainted our Baldwin in a Bicentennial scheme and added a super spark arrester in deference to the explosive atmosphere around a flour mill. Bryan Griebenow photographed the unnumbered unit on December 26, 1982.

Reputedly the busiest piece of trackage in Arizona, SP's Hayden Branch was running 24 hours per day when this picture was taken in the fifties. Right at milepost 1000, at Hayden Junction, Baldwin roadswitcher #5245 struggles to shove loads up two miles of 2.2% grade to the Kennecott smelter at Hayden. No air conditioning here, but later a more favorable grade was to replace this challenge.

(Richard Steinheimer)

1500 Horsepower Roadswitchers

Curiously, no locomotive builder other than Baldwin manufactured six-axle roadswitchers until 1951; for six years Eddystone had this market to itself. Beginning in September of 1946, Baldwin began shipping its A1A-A1A lightweights to Southern shortlines. A demonstrator, #1501, was built in February of 1948, and arrived at El Paso for Espee testing on April 10, 1948; within two months it brought home an order for fifteen roadswitchers. The A1A-A1A wheel arrangement allowed the locomotive's 131-ton weight to be spread over six axles—which in turn meant it could use trackage denied to 120-ton B-B units. The 11'6'' rigid truck wheelbase, potentially a problem on tight curves, was dealt with by slightly narrowing the flange gauge!

SP asked for three of the A1A-A1A model DRS-6-4-1500 (#5200-5202) and a dozen of the then-unseen C-C variant. Two of the latter were to become T&NO #187-188, while the remainder would be SP #5203-5212. The Baldwin roadswitcher era on SP rails began August 22, 1948, at Albany, Oregon. The #5200 was sent around the system to test possible operating locations; its picture at San Jose in September of 1948 appears on page 56 of the 1981 SP REVIEW.

The prime mover was an eight-cylinder 600-series, built with turbocharging to provide 1500 net horsepower. Ample copper in the Westinghouse #471 generator and #370 traction motors guaranteed that the electricals would be understressed. All these features were common to both the four-motor and six-motor units, which differed primarily in trucks and electrical connections for the additional traction motors. The six-motor units, however, were ballasted up to 165 tons, yielding 28 tons per axle.

Deliveries began with #5200 in August of 1948, followed in December by #5201-02. In March of 1949, Baldwin shipped T&NO #187-188 and SP #5203-05. SP units #5206-5212 all left Eddystone between April 23rd and June 1 of 1949.

As built, #5200-5202 and the first C-C units came with radiator air intakes low on the hood sides. Twenty years later, SP was to ask for this feature on SD45-2 units, but on the Baldwins it often meant rain and slush from the runningboards getting into the traction motor blowers. The solution by 1950 was to cut new grille openings directly above and block the lower ones from the inside (note that the T&NO totally plated theirs over). By the next order, Baldwin had revised its design.

SP began its own program of modifications very quickly. All fifteen units were initially painted with orange stripes on the hood ends, but in the interests of better visibility, solid aluminum paint was applied there. Another early change was to move the train number indicator back along the hood as time passed. In 1951, El Paso General Shops applied a BF-44 turbocharger to #5202, raising its horsepower to 1600; many of the early C-Cs were to receive this modification as well. It was decided in 1953 to convert #5200-5202 to multiple-unit operation. Painting was further modified after 1954, when SP began painting roadswitchers in "black widow" road unit colors. Five years later, SP's standard colors were revised to grey and scarlet; most of the early Baldwins received the new paint before retirement.

In the early fifties, assignments settled down to a pattern: #5200-01 in Oregon and #5202 on the Rio Grande Divison, with C-Cs distributed 5:4:1 among the Los Angeles, Tucson, and Sacramento Divisions. Late in that decade, #5200-5202 would all congregate at Douglas, Arizona, to replace the last standard gauge SP steam on the Nacozari Railway.

Attrition began in June, 1961, when #5209 was destroyed in a wreck and fire at Taylor Yard in Los Angeles. Programmed writeoffs began in 1963, when #5203, 04, 07, 10, and 11 were traded to GE, which in turn sold #5204 and 5207 to the McCloud

Entering service on August 22, 1948, Southern Pacific's first hood unit, Baldwin A1A-A1A #5200, had just received new aluminum hood-end paint in this view at Portland eleven months later. Only three, #5200-5202, carried even axle spacing to indicate lack of a center traction motor; so far, neither radiator air-intake placement nor train number indicators have been modified. *(D. H. Roberts:Best collection)*

Our #5200 was rebuilt at Brooklyn Roundhouse in September of 1953 with Baldwin's pneumatic multiple-unit connections; a year later it received black widow paint, as seen at Salem. The apparent air-intake area is double what it was in 1949, and the train number indicators have been moved back. Baldwin was still casting its bell hangers when #5200 was erected in 1948. *(Joel Barber)*

In their later years, the #5200-5202 migrated down to the border, replacing the last Ferrocarril de Nacozari steam (three SP 3400-series 2-8-0's) in 1959. In grey, with M.U. and a rear-facing horn, #5201 is pictured at El Paso on May 8, 1965. Nacozari rails (and Baldwins #5200-5201) were to be sold to the Mexican government in just three more months. *(F. H. Worsfold:Griebenow collection)*

We have not been able to locate a quality photograph of one of the A1A's after they were handed over to Mexico, but here is a "serviceable" view of #5200 at the Pacifico shops in Empalme on August 21, 1969. The short hood has a fuel filler for the "doghouse" reserve fuel tank inside; that is definitely NOT a steam generator exhaust stack! In December of 1969, this engine would become Chihuahua-Pacifico #400; it was scrapped in 1972. *(W. C. Whittaker:Harrison collection)*

30

1500 Horsepower Roadswitchers

The builder's portrait of C-C #5203 illustrates the DERS-2 class (#5203- 5212; later DF-101) in mint condition, complete with striping on the hood ends. Unlike later classes, this group of ten was built with General Steel Castings cast frames; uneven axle spacing accomodates three traction motors per truck. Radiator air intakes are low, and the number indicator is rather far forward. By this date (about March 5, 1949), Baldwin was using sheet steel for bell brackets. *(H. L. Broadbelt collection)*

Evolution and customer modifications (with factory kits) were necessary on the roadswitchers, too. Here's #5204 at Gerber, California, on June 11, 1951, a little more than two years old—with a new, higher radiator air intake, and metal cutout letters across the grille. The hood ends have been repainted in aluminum, and the class is now DF-101. This unit was sold for parts in March of 1964 to the McCloud River Railroad. *(Ray Whitaker collection)*

By 1957, still more changes had overtaken the ten DF-101 engines. At Taylor yard in February, #5203 models an abbreviated version of SP's "Black Widow" paint, with truncated orange stripes that do not reach back over the intake grilles. Only these GSC cast-frame units had a gusset at the stepwells. #5203 also has an extended stack, rear-mounted train number indicators, and a "radio equipped" logo on the hood. *(F. C. Smith: Youell collection)*

A dutiful SP painter did his best to bring the orange nose stripes around on #5212, but he wasn't entirely successful. Lettering has been moved back on this side, so that metal cutouts need not be used. An interesting oval stack has been applied in consequence of an upgrading to 1600 horsepower. #5212 sits out the afternoon commute rush at Millbrae with steel-underframe caboose #526 in August, 1957.
(Ray Whitaker collection)

Over on the T&NO, they took more drastic steps to remedy radiator intake problems; the old low intake has been completely plated over. Reclassified DS-300, the #188 was originally identical to #5203-5212. It was photographed at Fort Worth on May 22, 1965, only three months before tradein to Alco. A typical T&NO modification of the bell bracket moves it out of the way. *(Joe McMillan)*

Stored in anticipation of future restoration, the #5208 was given to the Railway & Locomotive Historical Society in 1969, when it became plain that the first generation of SP diesels would otherwise disappear completely. With faded grey paint, capped stack, and double radiator air intakes, it is by default the last SP Baldwin roadswitcher. In 1985, work began to return it to a pristine state.
(California State Railroad Museum)

T&NO #189 and 190 were the only two of their class, originally DERS-3, built in December of 1949. The factory photo, dated about December 7th, proves that hood-end stripes for roadswitchers were already history. The air intake location has been revised, the bell is down low, and there are no train number indicators. *(Southern Pacific collection)*

A generation of paint jobs and six years after the picture above, #190 works an endless cut at Ennis, Texas. By now, the bell has been moved back and up to T&NO's preferred location, and a small beacon light has been added atop the cab. None of T&NO's Baldwin roadswitchers ever had multiple-unit connections or dynamic brakes. The #190 was scrapped by Brazos Engineering for Alco in February of 1966, giving SP some credit toward a new Century-630. *(Lamar Kemp:Seay collection)*

River. In 1964, #5212 went to Precision Engineering. The newly-nationalized Nacozari bought #5200-01 in August of 1965; they eventually went to the Chihuahua-Pacific. The #5202 and 5206 were traded to EMD that same year, with #5205 following in 1966. That left #5208, which was donated to the Pacific Coast Chapter of the Railway & Locomotive Historical Society in December, 1969. It is now part of the California State Railroad Museum collection and is being restored to its original colors.

Another order was immediately placed for sixteen additional DRS-6-6-1500 C-C units, to be built in three configurations. In late 1949, Baldwin shipped T&NO #189-190 and SP #5213-5217, which were built with welded frames; all but the T&NO's came with dynamic brakes with round fan housings. Radiator inlets were high on the hood. In January of 1950, the order was continued with #5218-5226 and B-unit #5227; however, SP requested multiple-unit connections for this group.

Aluminum-painted ends were specified, and train number indicators placed midway along the hood. After delivery in January, #5213-5217 were leased in September of 1950 to the Northwestern Pacific, as the NWP's first road diesels. The DF-104's,

#5218-5226, were intended for use in multiple on Oregon branches, with the B-unit an experiment to see if cabs were always necessary. Avondale Yard was home base for T&NO's #187-190, where they were assigned to transfer drags across the Huey P. Long Bridge to New Orleans.

Early in 1951, B-unit #5227 was renumbered to #5500 to keep cabless units in a separate series; in 1955 the entire booster series was again renumbered to the 4900's to make room for more Alco RSD-5 units. New EMD SD7 units arriving in 1952 and 1953 bumped the Baldwins from Northwestern Pacific assignments; #5213- 5217 moved to West Oakland. Of all the latter 1500's, only #5213 was regularly used in Los Angeles.

Modifications were mainly invisible, such as the uprating of #5221, 5223-24, and 5226 to 1600 horsepower in the early fifties. One noticeable change was a gradual and incomplete conversion to dual sealed-beam headlights. Dynamic brakes on #5218-5220 were deactivated in 1963; certainly this feature saw little use on other units in later years. Most were repainted in "black widow," but only a few were redone in grey and scarlet.

The first to be retired was #5221, wrecked in a collision at Albany, Oregon, in April of 1959. It was

The five DERS-4/DF-103 engines, #5213-5217, were ordered for road service on the hilly Northwestern Pacific and hence came equipped with dynamic brakes. They worked in that assignment from September of 1950 until replaced by SD7's in January of 1953. On September 19, 1958, #5216 switches sugar beets at the Holly mill in Alvarado, California. The dynamics, with their round fan, take up most of the space in the short hood; there's no longer room for fuel there. *(Don Hansen)*

On a cab hop with steel-underframe caboose #108 at Pleasanton on November 6, 1958, #5214 shows off its replacement dual-element sealed beam headlight and high-level air intake. A heavy grille protects the roof radiators. Baldwin roadswitchers were common in the Bay Area during the fifties, but were gradually withdrawn to Roseville and Los Angeles as they grew older. *(Don Hansen)*

Operating "backward," with short hood forward, the #5214 rumbles through Elmhurst—in the East Bay south of Oakland—with a heavy transfer for the Santa Clara Yards on September 23, 1958. Roadswitchers numbered 5213 and up were built with Baldwin welded frames. Dynamic brakes are obvious here, as the fireman reaches for his orders. *(Don Hansen)*

Two days after the picture above, #5213 is nattily attired in black-and-orange "halloween" colors while switching at East Bank Junction in Los Angeles. A few engines of every class received this paint scheme in the summer of 1958. A tool box has been added behind the cab, while a thoughtful box for spare knuckles appears over the coupler. These big Baldwins found considerable favor in Los Angeles. *(Ken Douglas)*

Both ready to go to Electro-Motive as trades in October of 1968, #5217 and T&NO #600 sit dead on Roseville's rip track. Like #5213 above, #5217 has received a rear-porch tool box, and has been repainted in grey with full scarlet wings. This engine had, by 1968, outlasted all the other DF-103's by more than two years. *(Herman Friedrich:Towler collection)*

Another new Baldwin for Southern Pacific...at Aurant Yard in Los Angeles on February 12, 1950, #5220 will be set up for service at Portland on the 20th. Headlight, train indicators, and dynamic brake grids are all covered; a messenger rides in the cab. These DF-104's, #5218-5226, were purchased with dynamic brakes and multiple-unit connections for Oregon assignments. *(William Bassler)*

On April 7, 1951, #5221 was just another Baldwin roadswitcher at SP's Brooklyn roundhouse in Portland. However, in exactly eight more years, the #5221 would be demolished in a collision at Albany, Oregon in April of 1959—and be cut up for scrap at Sacramento on June 21, 1959. It thus became the first SP Baldwin to meet the torch. *(David Wilkie)*

In bright sunlight, the orange numerals and initials beside #5225's headlight almost fade away against an aluminum-painted hood end. The front gangway is down, and pneumatic multiple-unit connections (a Baldwin exclusive) have yet to be moved up onto a manifold. At Brooklyn in March of 1950, DERS-5 #5225 is just a few days old. *(D. H. Roberts:Dunscomb collection)*

A cow-and-calf road unit combination is pictured on Eddystone's grounds about January 31, 1950. Class DERS-5 and -6 #5226 and 5227 are identical except for the lack of a cab on the latter; dual fans for the dynamic brakes are obvious on the hood of #5227. Espee never painted its Baldwin B-units with large road numbers, even in their later years. *(H. L. Broadbelt collection)*

A small crowd has gathered for the first start-up of #5226-5227 at Brooklyn Roundhouse on March 2, 1950. With a few minor adjustments left to perform, Oregon's newest-technology locomotive will soon be out on the road. The #5227 would be renumbered to #5500 on January 18, 1951 and to #4900 in September of 1955. At left, ignored at the moment, is 0-6-0 #1130, which would work in this neighborhood until the summer of 1951. *(D. H. Roberts:Dunscomb collection)*

Less than a year away from retirement, the #4900 (originally #5227, then #5500) has been unbuttoned for inspection at the Eugene enginehouse in September of 1968. The right "cab" side has swing-open panels covering important gauges and hostling controls, while multiple-unit air connections have been moved up between dual gangways. The AS-616 in the background has a thicker, welded frame. *(Henry W. Brueckman)*

37

Espee's photographer got a little carried away with his wide-angle lens on the view camera, nipping off a bit of the "front" footboards of #5219 in this Oregon view in approximately 1956. A solid train of skeleton log bogies was the occasion for this picture, which incidentally shows off the Baldwin's beveled frame corners, latter-day pneumatic multiple-unit manifold, and round brake fan housings.

(James H. Harrison collection)

scrapped at Sacramento that June. GE took #5215-16 in trade for U25B's in November of 1963, while #5214 met the same fate three months later. T&NO #189-190 and SP #5213, 5222-23, and 5225 were all traded to EMD and Alco in 1966. The re-maining units all were sold in trade to EMD, which had them scrapped by Associated Metals at Benicia, California: (1967) #5224, 5226; (1968) #5217; (1969) #4900, 5220; and (1970) #5218 and 5219. None were resold for further service.

A decade later, #5219 has been banished forever from road assignments, but still lends its considerable tractive effort to the Eugene hump in this photo on December 17, 1966. Idler flat SPMW #5477 carries longitudinal piping for all multiple unit functions between #5219 and #4901, incidentally reducing the bridge loading of this powerful combination on some weak rail. A hump radio has been added, but compare the smooth, fan-less short hood to the view above; dynamic brakes are completely gone.

(David C. Lustig)

The AS-616 Roadswitchers

Numerous design improvements were made by Baldwin in 1950; a boost of 100 horsepower (to 1600) provided incentive for a new designation as AS-616, although appearances were unchanged. Southern Pacific was the first customer, ordering twelve early in 1950 on the basis of experience with the 1500-horsepower units.

These units were actually ordered as SP #5228-5229, San Diego & Arizona Eastern #200-201, and Northwestern Pacific #300-307, but the order was changed before construction began. Baldwin began shipping the new class DERS-7 (DF-106) units on August 17, 1950; the last left Eddystone on September 6. They were equipped with dynamic brakes but no multiple-unit connections.

Even though denied subsidiary-road numbers, #5233-5234 were leased to the SD&AE, while #5237-5239 went to work on the NWP upon arrival in September of 1950. In 1952, #5233-5234 moved from SD&AE to the NWP. Multiple-unit controls were added to Portland Division's #5228-30, 5232, and 5234 in 1957.

By the sixties, #5228, 5230-5232, 5234, and 5238 resided in Texas, while #5236 worked throughout the Bay Area; #5233 was assigned to Los Angeles. Retirements began in August, 1964, when #5239 became Oregon & Northwestern #2 and #5237 went to EMD. In 1965 and 1966, Alco took #5231, 5234, and 5238 in trade, scrapping them at Brazos Engineering in Houston. Electro-Motive bought three in 1966-67: #5229, 5235, and 5236. El Paso scrap dealer W. Silver & Company bought #5232 and 5228 in 1967 and 1968, leaving #5233 to remain in switching service at Los Angeles until August of 1970, when it was sold to Chrome Crankshaft for GE trade credit. The #5233 became the very last Baldwin roadswitcher to operate on the Southern Pacific. Chrome attempted to find a buyer for #5233, but eventually stripped it for parts.

Another twelve were ordered for delivery between February and April of 1951 as #5240- 5249 and #5501-5502. The first eight were to be built with dynamic brakes but no m.u., while the last three would constitute a "herd" of one cab and two cabless units. Each variant was assigned a different class: DF-107, 108, and 110.

New Baldwin-Lima-Hamilton builder's plates first appeared on #5248, shipped on March 30, 1951. Deliveries included #5241 set up on the Pacific Electric in San Bernardino on March 27, 1951, while #5247-5248 were delivered directly to the SD&AE. The "herd" (#5249 and boosters #5501-5502) reported on May 22, 1951 at Willits, on the NWP.

SP concentrated its m.u.-equipped hood units in Oregon, so the 5240s fanned out to other locations. The #5242-5246 were assigned to ore trains on the Tucson Division. #5241 was equipped briefly with PE trolley poles, but returned from lease in June, 1952. Most 5240s ended their days switching in Los Angeles; however, #5247 was a perennial Roseville engine.

In September of 1960, the Trona Railway bought #5249; it became Trona #53. Next to go were nine lower-numbered 5240s, retired between 1967 and 1969. Five (#5241, 5244-45, 5248, and booster #4902) were traded to EMD in 1967 and 1969. The Purdy scrapyard at Ewing (north of Roseville) bought #5242 and 5247 in July of 1968, while #5246 and 5243 were sold in Texas in 1967 and 1968. The #5240 went to National Metals in September of 1968. Last of the group was booster #4901, which was retired from the Eugene hump in 1970, and scrapped by Associated Metals at Benicia.

SP ordered a test batch of six AS-616 units with

SP's first order for AS-616's (and the first of this model for their builder) was for #5228-5239. The first two were to become SP, but the next two were to be SD&AE #200-201; the last eight were planned as NWP #300-307. Regrettably, plans were changed before construction. Built in August and September of 1950, this initial order is visually identical with its 1500-hp. predecessors, except for a change to sealed-beam headlights. At Gerber, California, February, 1956. *(Al Phelps:Shine collection)*

Back at the turn of the century, SP steam locomotives were fitted with exhaust "splitters" on their stacks to protect the wooden roofs of the snowsheds....the idea apparently still had some merit in 1955, when DF-106 #5235 tried on a similar device at Roseville. This is the only photo we've ever seen of a Southern Pacific Y-stack Baldwin. "Black Widow" colors were fitted to this radiator arrangement.

(Ray Whitaker)

twenty-five tons of ballast to see if tonnage ratings could be improved when adhesive weight was increased; the builder was therefore asked to increase these units' loaded weight from 323,150 pounds to 377,150. Delivery in November of 1951 was requested for three heavyweight cab units, #5250-5252, and three matching booster units, #5503-5505.

By now, B-L-H was welding up AS-616 mainframes, resulting in a thicker frame edge, with a cutout to allow swing of the truck with its large brake cylinder. These six units also were equipped with both dynamic brakes and multiple-unit controls.

Dynamometer car tests began in January, 1952, soon after these units began service, on the Siskiyou Line between Ashland and Eugene. The tests indicated that ballasting would not improve the tonnage rating of a B-L-H roadswitcher: "under average conditions in this territory, sufficient rail adhesion to fully utilize the electrical limits of the traction motors cannot be obtained." The AS-616 had reached its limit; ballast alone couldn't improve its performance.

As rare a Baldwin diesel photo as the author has ever seen, Pacific Electric #5241 relaxes at San Bernardino in 1951 in ephemeral lettering and trolley poles. It carried this identity for but nine months—leased from September 18, 1951 to June 11, 1952! And, no, it is not going out on the Sunset; in PE's context, train #2 is the *San Bernardino Hauler.*　　　　　*(Don Hansen collection)*

Carded to leave the desert outpost of Mina, Nevada, at 10:30 a.m., the *Mina Local* (trains #605-606) took a leisurely eight hours to cover the 174 miles up to Reno. Five boxcars and a rider coach made up the train on September 9, 1953; incidents such as this—with DF-106 #5234 on the point—were about as close as SP Baldwins came to regular "passenger service." *(Al Phelps:Whittaker collection)*

The class DF-109 cab units and DF-111 boosters were initially assigned to Portland Division branchlines. In September of 1955, the 5500-series boosters were renumbered to the 4900 series. By the later fifties, all six were in road service, but soon found permanent homes on the humps at Roseville and Englewood. Most of the heavyweights were regeared in their later years, from original 63:15 gearing and a theoretical 60 m.p.h. maximum speed to a slower 68:15 ratio, which reduced both top speed and minimum continuous speed, enhancing their value as hump units.

Booster #4904 was lost when a three-unit set of Baldwins ran through an open drawbridge on the Napa River in Northern California in 1959; it and #5260-61 were scrapped later that year. In the fall of 1961, Kaiser Bauxite in Jamaica bought #5250 and 5251, delivering them to its isolated railhead via a converted Navy landing ship. They became KBCo. #106 and 105, as pictured in our 1981 REVIEW on page 75. The #4905 became an Alco trade in August of 1966, while #4903 and #5252 went to EMD in the spring of 1967. The #4903 was the last Baldwin B-unit in the United States.

Two young railfans wait for the action to begin as the Speno ballast- cleaning train is prepared for service at South San Francisco on January 31, 1959. An assignment such as this would typically be given to second- string locomotives, which is where the Baldwins quickly found themselves. The #5245, among others, carried temporary outside handrails at one time, but this feature wasn't universally applied.
(Don Hansen)

Fords and Plymouths share the pavement with DF-107 #5242 at First and Franklin Streets in Oakland on September 12, 1958. The big Baldwins, with their excellent low-speed traction, were well-suited to work on heavy transfer drags in urban areas, both in Los Angeles and the Bay Area. Most of the engines in this class received an oval spark-arrester stack in the mid-fifties. *(Don Hansen)*

Espee was an enthusiastic purchaser of Baldwin diesels until 1953, when it became apparent to management that Alco, EMD, and Fairbanks-Morse were beginning to build locomotives of competitive performance and more "maintainability." One of the interlopers, GP9 #5701, compares its profile to that of #5242 in 1958. *(W. C. Whittaker)*

#5242 again, this time in grey and scarlet wings, working a cut of tri-level auto racks on June 28, 1965. The location is where North Main Street crosses the Los Angeles River; tracks here are in place on both banks of the concrete watercourse. The 1951-vintage AS-616 still had three years to go before scrapping by Purdy Brothers at Ewing, California. *(Ken Douglas)*

#5245 shows off its new coat of grey paint at the throat tracks into Los Angeles Union Passenger Terminal on January 3, 1968; the ridgeline to the right marks the parking lot for Dodger Stadium. SP was inconsistent in painting its Baldwin roadswitchers with scarlet wings on the nose; many units never received this visual treatment. This unit was rebuilt in 1957 with a modified turbosupercharger, which actually reduced its horsepower output back to 1500. *(Tom Hotchkiss)*

An interesting lineup like this probably was rare in real life, but Baldwin's photographer preserved for us an image of a "herd:" #5501, 5502, and 5249 just prior to shipment on April 28, 1951. The #5249 was the only engine in class DF-108, and the two AS-616B's were the only two DF-110's; they were the last of this model with thin frame edges. Another picture of this set in transit appears in *SP REVIEW 1952-82* on page 13. *(H. L. Broadbelt collection)*

Espee painters at Taylor Roundhouse in Los Angeles work on a custom job for locomotive dealer Industrial Railway Equipment Company in November of 1964. Baldwin AS-616 #5239 has been overhauled and sold to the Oregon & Northwestern as their #2; finishing touches on its yellow-and-red paint are being completed. Only #5239 and #5249 of the "thin frame" AS-616's went on to second owners. *(David C. Lustig)*

After only nine years of service, DF-108 #5249 was sold in September of 1960 to the Trona Railway, northeast of Mojave in California's High Desert. Considerably modified by its later owner (a strong believer in Baldwin diesel technology), Trona #53 was still operating a decade after its brethren on the SP had been sold off; here it is at Trona on January 30, 1979. *(Mark Denis)*

By 1951, evolution caught up with the AS-616; all three of B-L-H's competitors were on the verge of announcing C-C roadswitcher models. Electro-Motive was finishing a demonstrator to back up previous proposals for a six-axle "super GP7" with performance to match that of the AS-616. Simultaneously, Alco introduced its RSD-4 and Fairbanks-Morse brought out the H16-66. Both the C&NW and C&O, senior customers for the AS-616, promptly switched allegiance.

Southern Pacific during this period was faced with the problem of needing new diesels for seasonal peaks, and would place orders almost on speculation, to see if the builders actually could deliver when promised—not an easy task in those days. In fact, SP twice asked EMD for GP7 units, in 1948 and 1949, but cancelled both orders in favor of earlier deliveries from Baldwin. (EMD order #5013, placed by SP on November 23, 1948, was for 28 GP7 units; they would have borne construction numbers 9387-9414.)

Although EMD's first SD7 demonstrator, the #990, was completed in May of 1951, SP wanted to perform extensive road testing of its new quad-mount truck before placing an order. At this point in time, opposed-piston F-M engines were unknown on the SP, and Alco's RSD-4 didn't have an adequate main generator. (Alco began production of the RSD-5, with a large GT-566 generator, in March of 1952.) SP wanted thirty-four "known quantity" units for delivery in the early months of 1952; as a result, the order went to B-L-H. On February 21, 1952, however, the board of directors approved a new round of orders that included both the SD-7 and RSD-5; the AS-616 had been compared with its competition and found wanting.

The final SP order for B-L-H roadswitchers was divided among class DF-112 for the Pacific Lines as #5253-5278, and class DF-113 for the T&NO as #177-184; there were, however, many variations within these two groups.

First to be shipped were the T&NO units, which left Eddystone in January of 1952. None were fitted with dynamic brakes, but #182-183 did carry steam generators. (This feature didn't last long; so far no picture has surfaced showing a T&NO AS-616 pulling a passenger train—or even one proving that a steam generator was installed.)

Following the T&NO units were SP #5263-5271, shipped together on February 27, 1952. These were built first because they had the least options—just dynamic brakes. The next to be shipped were #5253-5259 in March and April, which were fitted with dynamics, pilot plows, and multiple-unit connections. The #5260-5262 came next, with dynamics and m.u., destined for immediate lease to the Oregon, California & Eastern, then owned jointly by SP and the Great Northern.

Four more, #5273-5276, followed in May, fitted with Pyle-National "Gyralites" in cowlings on the hood ends for service on the Pacific Electric and the San Diego & Arizona Eastern. These also had multiple-unit connections, apparent in our cover picture. The final two, #5277-5278, were ordered to dieselize SP's Placerville Branch, which was about to lose its outer-end turntable to highway construction. In consequence, they were built with dual-station cab controls as well as dynamic brakes—but lacked multiple-unit connections.

Roadswitchers in the fifties were assigned to divisions, instead of operating in pools as they do today; the twenty-six DF-112s were scattered around the

On a typically murky August morning in 1963, B-L-H AS-616 #5265 makes a delivery of ballast via Union Pacific trackage on the east side of the Los Angeles River (bypassing street running on SP's own rails). These six- motor, 1600-hp. machines were used in heavy switching and transfer assignments, just as the 1500-series SD7's are today. Note the recessed dynamic brake fans on the short hood.   *(Ken Douglas)*

In February through May of 1952, B-L-H delivered to SP its largest single order: twenty-six thick-frame AS-616's (#5253-5278) with a variety of options. By this time, the builder had deleted louvers on the hood bulge. Only #5253-5262 carried multiple unit connections without signal lights. In brand-new condition at Wells, Nevada on July 4, 1952, #5253 is part of a team of new helpers.   *(Ray Whitaker collection)*

In 1952, DF-112's #5253-5259 were assigned to the Salt Lake Division, principally for use as helpers on the stiff grades out of Wells, Nevada. Only a few months old in this picture dated May of 1952, #5255 is helping a 4300-series 4-8-2 with a very heavy second #28 at Wells. If that train doesn't look much like the *San Francisco Overland*, there's good reason: it is really an eastbound troop train, running on the streamliner's schedule authority.
(Al Phelps:Shine collection)

Pacific Lines upon their arrival. Neither the Western nor San Joaquin Divisions needed any, and only one went to the Coast. The largest initial assignment was to the Salt Lake Division, which obtained the seven with pilot plows, #5253-5259, for helper duties in the Nevada desert. Another four were assigned to the Rio Grande Divison for mine branches. Three each worked the NWP, PE, and the Portland Division, while #5277-5278 were diverted from Placerville to San Diego. The Sacramento Division got two, #5271-5272, while Los Angeles then only "owned" one...the #5270.

By the later sixties, assignments had changed dramatically. The #5257, 5274, and 5276 had moved to Texas, while Los Angeles was considered "home port" to #5254, 5258-59, 5265, and 5272. The #5256 and 5266 were both used in Oregon. Most of the rest ended their days working at various yards between West Oakland and Roseville on the Western and Sacramento Divisions.

Retirements began in a dramatic fashion in July of 1959, when the multiple set of #5260, 4904, and 5261 plunged through an open drawbridge over the Napa River. They were stripped at Bayshore, and

Operating northbound through Hopland, California, on June 21, 1952, month-old AS-616 #5262 is on lease to the Northwestern Pacific, where it will serve for a relatively brief six months before replacement by new SD7's (which were always more comfortable in road service). By this late date, most of NWP's through freight service was handled by SP diesels, rendering the water tower useless.
(Fred H. Matthews)

The most obviously specialized of all the AS-616 units were #5273-5276, built with large Pyle-National "Gyralites" faired into their hoods. This feature was intended for street running on the Pacific Electric's Northern District to San Bernardino. Three were delivered brand-new to the PE, and #5276 followed sixteen months later. All were returned to SP by February of 1954. Here are #5275 and 5274 at San Bernardino in the summer of 1952. *(Jack Whitmeyer:Smith collection)*

dismantled a few months later. The #5273 and #5275 were the first to leave the roster intact, being sold in late 1961 to Rayonier for logging near Gray's Harbor, Washington. In 1963, General Electric bought #5253 for protection power on the new Oro-Dam Railway, but immediately resold it to the McCloud River as their #34. (McCloud in turn sold it to Oregon & Northwestern #4 in 1970.)

Routine scrapping began in 1964, when #5265 was traded to EMD, followed in 1965 by #180, 5269, and

5271. The #178 was traded to GE in 1967, while Rayonier bought #5272 that same year. In 1968, three more were sold for service: #5257 to the Roscoe, Snyder & Pacific; #5274 to Oregon & Northwestern; and #5276 to Rayonier. Routine retirements that year included #179, 181, 182, 5263, 5268, and 5277, cut up in Texas and California.

The market for secondhand Baldwin roadswitchers was saturated by this time, and no SP units were sold for service after June of 1968. In 1969, all

#5268 drills a cut under the old Adeline Avenue bridge in West Oakland on June 7, 1960. Note that #5263-5272 and #5277-5278 were never equipped with multiple-unit connections—although the entire DF-112 group (#5253-5278) was fitted with dynamic brakes. This particular unit spent most of its years in Northern California, being scrapped at Benicia for credit toward a new SD45 in December of 1968. *(Don Hansen)*

It's easy to think of the AS-616B units as confined solely to hump duties, since throughout the sixties that was their principal assignment, but in fact they were used in road service for many years. Few pictures have surfaced illustrating these earlier times, but Don Hansen got lucky in October of 1958 at First and Oak Streets in Oakland, as #5260 and 4903 moved into his viewfinder. Within a year, #5260 would be destroyed in a spectacular bridge accident.

remaining 1952- built units were to be vacated from the roster. The #177 and 183 were scrapped in Texas, while #184 went to LaGrange for disposal. On the Pacific Lines, the last eleven DF-112s were traded to EMD between March and November of 1969; they were actually scrapped at Associated Metals in Benicia, California. The last two were the #5266 and 5270, sold on November 26, 1969.

COLLATERAL READING ON BALDWIN DIESELS:

Dolzall, Gary W. DIESELS FROM EDDYSTONE. Kalmbach Books, 1984

Kirkland, John F. DAWN OF THE DIESEL AGE. Interurban Press, 1983

Pinkepank, Jerry A. THE SECOND DIESEL SPOTTER'S GUIDE. Kalmbach Books, 1973

Strapac, Joseph A. COTTON BELT LOCOMOTIVES. Shade Tree Books, 1977

Neither the weather nor the future was bright for two aging warhorses at the south end of Dunsmuir Yard in January of 1964. Matched sets of F7's, such as this one led by #6332, were soon to be replaced by GP35's, and Baldwin AS-616's would gradually migrate to Roseville or Los Angeles. South end switcher #5266 erupts a puff of dark smoke amid snow and slush. *(Don Hansen)*

The most important of SP's many "little yards" around Los Angeles was Butte Street Yard, officially a Pacific Electric facility, but actually the key to SP and PE branches to both south and west. It was also the main interchange point for Union Pacific traffic. At the top end, on December 26, 1959, a few blocks from better-known Redondo Junction, #5269 hauls dead SW8 #4612 across Santa Fe Avenue.

(Ken Douglas)

The assigned Woodland switcher on January 1, 1961 was AS-616 #5264 in Halloween paint, laying over for the holiday with class C-30-6 bay window caboose #1338. Woodland is an agricultural community west of Sacramento; locomotives assigned here report to Roseville for regular maintenance. Black and orange paint was applied to only a minority of DF-112 engines.

(Don Hansen)

With the advent of scarlet and grey paint in 1958-59, SP faced a minor dilemma with its Baldwin roadswitchers: the red "wings" were a bit too tall to fit under the radiator intakes—thus were often deleted in repainting. At the upper end of Taylor Yard in Los Angeles on an overcast May 12, 1969, #5254 illustrates this particular economy. Perhaps of more interest is the set of non-standard outside handrails, added when the locomotive was on lease to Kaiser Steel's Eagle Mountain Railroad.

(Ernie Towler collection)

49

The Texas & New Orleans was still a "separate" railroad in 1952, and specified its AS-616's differently from those of the Pacific Lines— since #179 carried no dynamic brakes, it was fitted with an auxiliary short-hood fuel tank like those on early SP Baldwins. Another consequence of no dynamics was that the classification lights were mounted lower on the short hood. Unlike the DF-112's, DF-113 units #177-184 had a battery- box step behind the cab.

(Southern Pacific collection)

At the Port Terminal Railroad Authority enginehouse at the Houston Ship Channel on April 30, 1955, AS-616 #184 shares layover time with a Missouri Pacific S-12 of similar vintage. As on the 1500-horsepower roadswitchers, T&NO shop forces routinely moved AS-616 bells upward and back from above the headlight. Its DF-113 class had been changed to DS-302 by the time of this picture.

(Joe Dale Morris collection)

Heavyweight AS-616B #5504 was photographed at the builder's Eddystone Works on October 19, 1951. The three DF-111 units, #5503-5505, weighed 375,000 pounds, twenty-five tons more than their more common relatives. All the 5500's were renumbered in September of 1955 to the 4900 series in order to make room for anticipated Alco RSD-5 units; this particular Baldwin was to be lost in the Napa River accident less than eight years after delivery. *(H. L. Broadbelt collection)*

In deference to its usual full-throttle, low-speed operation on the torrid Roseville hump, heavyweight AS-616B #4905 has been given some additional louvers below the standard radiator air intakes. Sets of three Baldwins were favored hump power for over a decade at all three of Espee's biggest yards at Houston, Los Angeles, and Roseville. Standard practice with black widow colors on cabless units was to forego "wings" on the front hood. *(Ray Whitaker collection)*

A little routine maintenance sidelines hump pusher #4901 at the Eugene roundhouse on March 9, 1967, allowing a close-up photo of some details. By this date, all three ballasted, thick-frame B's (#4903-4905) had been retired, leaving two thin-frame AS-616B and one 1500B as the entire fleet. This unit, now painted with a larger number and a Forest-Service approved spark arrester (indicated by the "bullet" over the road number), will be the last to go, serving until 1970. *(David C. Lustig)*

In this 1973 photo, ITT-Rayonier #70 displays a host of second-owner modifications applied after its arrival at Gray's Harbor, Washington in December of 1967 (where it was responsible for the demise of Rayonier's last steam). Once SP #5272, the #70 has its bell moved behind the radiator, a mast-mounted beacon added, and outside handrails applied. It even pulls a tender! *(Henry W. Brueckman)*

Central Texas shortline Roscoe, Snyder & Pacific purchased SP #5257 in January of 1968, adding an interesting beacon and an outside-hung fire extinguisher in the process. The big Baldwin's generally rundown condition and rigid trucks worked against its success on light rail, and it was sold for scrap in 1970. In fresh new paint, AS-616 #400 poses at the enginehouse in Roscoe on June 22, 1968. *(Joe McMillan)*

Seven-year-old Baldwins #4904, 5261, and 5260 ended their working years in spectacular fashion by diving from an open drawbridge near Napa, California, on July 12, 1959. Once the hulks were rescued from the water, they were taken to Bayshore Shops for survey and parts removal, as pictured on September 13th. All three were scrapped that November, sharing with #5221 the dubious honor of being the first Baldwins to leave the SP roster. *(Ray Whitaker collection)*

Tucked away in the El Paso roundhouse on its way to a date with the Baldwin Field Service Engineer who will put it in service on January 13, 1950. The headlight is soundly boxed in, and train number indicators are taped over.   (Gordon H. Motts; courtesy of Lyle Dautrich)

AS-616 #5247 was sold for scrap to the Purdy Company at Ewing (north of Roseville) in July of 1968, but its short hood lives on—still in SP paint—as the load tester for the Sierra Railroad Baldwin fleet! This relic still resides (at presstime) outside the SRR enginehouse at Oakdale, California, even though Sierra's own Baldwins are now dressed in green and white.   (Ted Benson)

The photographer was pleasantly surprised to find a new GP40-2, complete with a newly-introduced "SSW" initial on the nose, all by itself on the point of a Fresno-bound freight at Herndon, crossing the San Joaquin River bridge. On the other hand, with merger imminent, there can be nothing more ephemeral than the most-recently delivered SP/SSW units, which won't be around in these colors very much longer!

(Ted Benson)

New and Upgraded Units

In the last decade, Southern Pacific's carloadings have dropped by almost a third. New autos, auto parts, and forest products have all suffered from the recessionary economy and the influx of imports. Consequently, SP hasn't been buying the large annual quantities of diesel locomotives it once did. On the other hand, due to layoffs of maintenance personnel, SP has a current shortage of reliable units. One closely- watched index at One Market Plaza is the daily report of trains held awaiting power—a printout that often does not bring managerial smiles.

SP currently owns more units than it needs, but much of the excess is in smaller switchers and older road power. There aren't enough reliable, modern units available at major terminals to provide competitive service all the time. The logical move, then, was to replace old-timers with modern road freight units. It was decided to sell more than a hundred units for scrap and purchase new power from both builders.

General Electric was willing to take three old units in trade for each new B36-7, so SP assembled a "hospital train" of retired locomotive hulks, sending back to their builder most of the U28B, U28C, and U30C stored for years around Los Angeles. In November and December of 1984, GE shipped in return sixteen new 3600hp. B36-7 locomotives as SP #7754-7769, numbered below the 1980 deliveries. On a per-axle rating, the B36-7 units, with 900 horsepower at each axle, are SPs most powerful diesels ever.

Electro-Motive was asked for thirty-four GP40-2 units, evolved from the 7600 and 7900 series engines delivered between 1978 and 1980. Since the Cotton Belt has a higher percentage of net income than parent SP, it had more cash available; as a result, the order was divided 26 to the Cotton Belt and 8 to the SP. Delivery was ready to commence when SP asked EMD to ship the SSW units first, causing some complications with order numbers stamped on the frames. SSW #7248-7273 were shipped in October and November of 1984, followed in November by SP #7240-7247.

SP did not purchase GP50s, which would have been more compatible with those of the Santa Fe, because they could obtain GP40s sooner and at somewhat less cost. Neither group of locomotives carries the familiar L-shaped engineer's windshield, and mechanical oscillating signal lights have been replaced by "cross-eyed" strobes.

Unless the SP&SF merger does not take place, and an independent SP gains a new lease on life, these fifty diesels should be the final additions to the Southern Pacific roster. The very last new SP locomotive would then be B36-7 #7769, which entered service in December, 1984.

A more common occasion when SP will dispatch a train with but one unit is on the short-and-fast Sprints, which rarely are given even a thousand tons. New Cotton Belt GP40-2 #7269, eastbound through Walnut on June 9, 1985, is all alone with its abbreviated trainload of trailers for Phoenix; it helps to have a reliable new unit available for this service! *(Dave Crammer/Finer Enterprises)*

Extra 9291 west snakes into the "A" Yard at Taylor Yard, Los Angeles on March 24, 1983, with something a bit unusual in the consist. Four Southern Railway GP50's have been borrowed by EMD to show off their builder's latest technology; they'll demonstrate on the SP for a week. Although Santa Fe was impressed with GP50's, SP instead chose to buy GP40-2's when it placed an order for 34 units in 1984.

(Dick Stephenson)

General Electric #606, a new B36-8 demonstrator, leads SP B36-7's #7772, 7770, and 7773 through Minnow Siding, between Eugene and Oakridge, Oregon. The date is September 9, 1983, and SP has brought out its instrument car to evaluate GE's new microprocessor technology aboard the red-white-and-blue machine against its first cousins on a typical assignment. The #606 operated on the point for three days, and was used as the last unit on the fourth and final day. In spite of this visit (or perhaps because of it), SP decided to stick with GE's proven "dash-seven" electronics for its 1984 order of sixteen B36's.

(Charles R. Lange)

NEW LOCOMOTIVES 1982-1986

Numbers	Class	Builder's Model	Quantity	Delivery
7240-7247	EF430L-4	GP40-2	8	Nov. 84
7248-7273 (SSW)	EF430W-3	GP40-2	26	Oct. 84-Nov. 84
7754-7769	GF437L-2	B36-7	16	Nov. 84-Dec. 84
			50	

A new feature for SP units is the road initial and number painted on the buffer beam, Cotton Belt-style. In common with recent EMD deliveries (but a first for SP), these GP40-2's have the current-standard angled blower bulge behind the fireman on the hood side. One cherished SP tradition has died—no more L-shaped engineer's windshield. SP units #7240-7247, even though lower- numbered, were delivered after those of the Cotton Belt. *(Joe McMillan)*

The Cotton Belt GP40-2's, #7248-7273, are identical to SP's but for lettering. These are the very first hood units ever to display a large block "SSW" on their nose. At Corwith Yard in Chicago on November 6, 1984, #7256 has yet to touch home rails. The 26 SSW units were delivered in October and November of 1984, followed by SP #7240-7247. That GP35 behind is ominous; are these the last SP/SSW locomotives? *(Joe McMillan)*

EMD came up with its own version of a rear signal light cluster for the GP40-2's, eliminating the mechanical oscillating signal light and replacing it with strobe lights disposed at skewed angles. A large box is necessary to support the new light arrangement; of course SP has no need for classification lights in either high or low positions. At Santa Fe's Corwith Yard in Chicago upon delivery, October 26, 1984. *(Joe McMillan)*

The *Oakland-Los Angeles Trailers* is at the Allen Avenue Crossover between Burbank and Glendale, heading into the morning sun at 7:45 a.m. on February 5, 1985 with three-month-old GP40-2 #7247 (the highest-numbered Southern Pacific unit in the current order) in charge. The new units are already thoroughly mixed with older power and have been seen all over California. *(Ed Workman)*

Empties return to Los Angeles from Mojave on May 9, 1985 over the infrequently-used Soledad Canyon Line south of Palmdale. This particular location is between Humphries and Honby. A power shortage has caused SP to call some of its newest power for this drag assignment, placing new GP40-2's #7268 and 7244 ahead of #8300, 7322, and 9096. Cab roof air-conditioning is quite apparent here. *(Bruce Veary)*

For reasons unknown, both the GE and EMD orders for 1984 came without the familiar L-shaped engineer's windshield, but the GE units have backup horns.....never previously applied. Both orders have "cross-eyed strobes," rather than mechanical oscillating headlights—with each lens pointed in a different direction. Rear class lights and number boxes are passe'—and this is how GE disposes of them.

(Joseph A. Strapac)

The most powerful four-axle locomotives ever owned by SP are these sixteen B36-7 units from GE, with the power of an SD45 from sixteen cylinders. Major improvements in wheel-slip control allow these 140-ton units to maintain low-speed traction in spite of higher horepower per axle. They arrived in the fall of 1984 in trade for 48 old six-axle GE hulks from SP's "attic". Still fresh (even the stack is clean), #7759 pauses briefly at Santa Susana on January 10, 1985.   (Bruce Veary)

If Southern Pacific ordered F40PH's, no doubt they'd look like this! The California Department of Transportation bought eighteen silver cab units from EMD to replace leased SP units on commute trains....complete with head-end train "hotel" power, SP-standard light packages, air conditioning, plow pilots, and a set of horns guaranteed to get attention. Four new machines, yet to enter service, gleam in the afternoon sun at San Francisco on April 24, 1985.   (Ken Rattenne)

New General Electric B36-7 #7759 leads two older cousins through the famous Chatsworth Rocks in January of 1985. SP's experimental B36-7's of 1978, #7770-7773, carried noise-suppression baffles over the rear air intakes, but otherwise were very similar to the 1984 machines, numbered just below as #7754-7769. Santa Fe and Espee B36-7's will be grouped in the 8500 series if present plans succeed.

(Ed Workman)

In contrast with the diminutive *Sprint* trains pictured elsewhere in this chapter, a pair of new B36-7 units (#7768 and 7755) is on the point of the westbound *TUWCK* from Tucson on May 17, 1985 as the 98-car train fights momentum down Beaumont Hill on the last lap into West Colton between Ordway and El Casco. Three six-axle units are entrained two-thirds of the way back, to help keep 8255 tons under control.

(Bruce Veary)

It seems reasonable to use the very newest units on the railroad's hottest train: here is SP's Phoenix-City of Industry *Sprint* train, ten flatcars of loaded trailers, no empties, and no caboose, breezing through Guasti near Pomona close to the end of its run. This service is designed to compete directly with trucks on the paralleling Interstate #10. In charge of only 561 tons are GP40-2's #7269 and 7948.

(Bruce Veary)

UPGRADED LOCOMOTIVES 1982-1986

Numbers	Class	Builder's Model	Quantity	Delivery
1610-1613	GF400R-1	TEBU (Road Slug)	4	Jan. 82-May 82
7422-7464	EF632R-2	SD45	43	Jan. 82-Dec. 82
7465-7488	EF632R-2	SD45	24	Jan. 83-Dec. 83
7489-7536	EF632R-2	SD45	48	Jan. 84-Dec. 84
7537-7560	EF632R-2	SD45	24	Jan. 85-Dec. 85
7561-7566	EF632R-2	SD45	6	Jan. 86-Mar. 85
7960-7967 (SSW)	EF430CR-1	GP40	8	Jan. 82-Jun. 82
9500-9525	*EF636R-1	SD45T-2	26	Apr. 86-Dec. 86
			183	

*Locomotives scheduled for upgrading at Sacramento as of presstime.

Meanwhile, Sacramento Locomotive Works continues to turn out better-than-new SD45 rebuilds at a pace of two per month; by the end of 1985, the series will reach #7560. This one, at Los Angeles on June 1, 1985, was formerly #8906, released for service a few weeks previously on April 26th. Yes, it also has the new strobe signal lights; classification light openings on the short hood were plated over prior to repainting.

(Joseph A. Strapac)

At Eagle Lake, Texas, on July 30, 1983, Espee's San Antonio-Houston SAHOY has been given an all-Katy consist. Beginning with GP40 #173, then leased Conrail GP38-2 #8236, then GP40 #226, road slug #501, GP40 #227, and GP40 #174, the engines are balancing off horsepower-hours loaned by Southern Pacific.

(Charles Howard)

SD40T-2's #8496, 8489, and 8492 are led by Santa Fe "snoot" #5140 southbound down the Rio Grande Valley at Sabinal, New Mexico on the Santa Fe's New Mexico Division. Engines are combined for the Cochise Coal Train, which operates over the tracks of both railroads, on a warm September 6, 1981. In 1986 or 1987, these engines will all be painted the same color and carry numbers in the 5800 and 6000 series.
(John C. Lucas)

Neither Missouri Pacific SD40 #3016 nor Southern Pacific SD40T-2 #8300 is at home here; we're overlooking the Southern Railway yard in New Orleans on June 21, 1978, as the two EMD's prepare to deliver westbound tonnage to Houston. All three roads exchange power here to some extent, and many off-line locomotive colors are seen on the SP as far west as El Paso.
(Michael Palmieri)

SD45T-2 #9218 combines with four Burlington Northern locomotives to pilot an empty SATX train from San Antonio meeting a U30C on the point of a loaded coal train on the siding at Des Moines, New Mexico in June of 1983. This is BN (Colorado & Southern) trackage here; it sees considerable southbound coal traffic using pool power from many roads.
(Chris Raught)

In another portent of events to come, four Santa Fe units, led by 1974- vintage U36C #8761, detour over the SP through Fresno (at Belmont Avenue on June 15, 1984) with train #1-991-15. Eight AT&SF trains took this route from Stockton to Bakersfield because of a derailment. After the merger, this sight will be common, since SP&SF intends to abandon the present Santa Fe tracks on Fresno streets—but the U36C's will be 9500's.
(Glen Icanberry)

Where are we? The bridge is lettered for Santa Fe, but no AT&SF power is in evidence as Burlington Northern SD45 #6408 locks couplers with SP U33C #8719 and SD40 #8458 to haul southbound tonnage over Santa Fe Joint Line track at Larkspur, Colorado. This picture is dated February 28, 1979, when U33C's were still commonly traded with the BN; now SP #8719 awaits its fate in the dead line and #8458 has been rebuilt to #7365.

(Steve Patterson)

Only rarely does pool power move eastbound on SP's Coast Line, and almost none of it gets the point position. Here's a happy exception as Rio Grande SD40T-2 #5381 leads SP #7330, 9251, and 8960 past the old cattle- loading point of Strathearn, California (just west of Simi Valley), on June 7, 1985.

(Bruce Veary)

Southern Pacific B30-7 #7876 awaits departure from Espee's Avondale Yard near New Orleans in company with Southern Railway SD45's #3154 and 3150. Southern power usually runs through as far as Houston, where it is turned back toward home rails. We've yet to see pictures of the corollary—SP units deep in Southern territory.
(Gerald Sires)

An empty unit coal train leaves Belen, New Mexico on the morning of August 27, 1982. Santa Fe SD40-2 #5126 leads SP SD40T-2's #8497 and 8490; midtrain helpers today are SP #8494 and 8495, with Santa Fe #8151. Each road has contributed a brace of modern SD40-2 units to a unit train service operated partially over the rails of each of them.
(Samuel L. Gonzales)

Great excitement was created within the Southern California enthusiast community when, in 1983-84, Milwaukee Road units began operating all the way through to Los Angeles on the the "Cotton Rock" from Kansas City. As demonstrated by SD40-2's #156 and 161 at the desert outpost of Fingal, California, in February of 1984, they occasionally even operated on the point.
(John Totten)

A colorful threesome leads the first section of the APLAA (auto parts for Los Angeles) through Muldoon, Texas on September 30, 1979. Chessie- painted Baltimore & Ohio GP40-2's #4188 and 4116 sandwich SP SD40T-2 #8388 in a scene no longer as common as it was a few years ago. *(Stuart Schroeder)*

This section might well be called "what railroad is it?" At Canon City, Colorado on July 19, 1983, five SP SD45T-2 tunnel motors operate eastbound on Rio Grande rails with freight from the Pacific Northwest taking a shortcut to Kansas City. An occasion when off-line locomotives are run accompanied on the Rio Grande is considered highly unusual, but the future will see more of this! *(Robert R. Harmen)*

Southern Pacific Graduates

We're at the Katy's Eureka Yard in Houston, Texas on an overcast Friday afternoon in July of 1983. A leased Morrison-Knudsen hybrid SD40 works with M-K-T SD40-2 #608 with an outbound freight; its cab, frame, and trucks are from wrecked SP SD45 #8820, scrapped by M-K, and the long hood is fabricated from one end of retired DD35 #9900. While a clever work of engineering, this type of project is less necessary during the present glut of used locomotives. *(Charles Howard)*

A vivid red-and-black prewar NW2 has worked for Ideal Cement at Portland, Colorado, since December of 1973. They purchased it from locomotive dealer Chrome Crankshaft, but it was originally SP #1317 and later #1911. Although 41 years of age in this August 1982 photo, the switcher is still earning its keep. *(Ed Fulcomer)*

The author admits a fondness for tiger-striped SP diesels; both California traction museums agree with this interest. The Orange Empire Railway Museum at Perris, California, acquired this Alco S-4 in 1978 from the Marine Corps, which had been using it for radar experiments. It was formerly SP #1802, but was restored in 1982-83 to its original colors of orange and black. See page 70 of our 1981 REVIEW for a view of a Northern California tiger-striper at a museum. *(Jim Walker)*

The California Western operates three former Espee Alco RS-11's (purchased in 1980) between Willits and Fort Bragg in Northern California. CW #63 and 62 (once SP #2935 and 2919) are leading the daily eastbound mixed train into Willits on March 9, 1982, as it stops to pick up a few loads. *(Bruce Evans)*

Bethlehem Steel in Vernon is gone now, but in December of 1982 this interesting comparison could be made between two SP graduates (SW-1 #1006 and S-6 #1229) and General Electric 25-tonner #17. Even though the two units on the left were considered very small for railroad duties, they dwarf the 150-horsepower machine! *(Bryan Griebenow)*

Slugging Away
With TEBU's

The rationale for using road slugs is tied to the concept of unit trains— in this case, a constant movement of bulk aggregate from inland quarries to distribution points around the Houston waterfront. A slow, heavy train needs considerable tractive effort and relatively little horsepower, demonstrated here by two GP40E's and a road slug (TEBU) performing the work of four GP35's. Gravel from San Antonio turns eastbound up the old San Antonio & Aransas Pass mainline to Houston from Tower 115 at Eagle Lake, Texas on September 12, 1983.

(Charles Howard)

Use of Tractive Effort Booster Units was originally proposed in SP circles for Arizona branches that consistently generate heavy train loads. General Electric had been promoting its MATE concept, finally sending a "demonstrator set" out west. SP bought the idea but not the hardware, going with EMD locomotives and homebuilt road slugs instead. Nine TEBU's were rebuilt at Sacramento in 1981. It's August 12, 1984, and the *Tucson-Nogales Manifest* is operating today with but five loads and caboose #1910. Two TEBU sets equal 12,000 horsepower for this train! *(J. R. Doughty)*

Road slugs are an idea only recently adopted by the Southern Pacific, but the concept has proved its worth wherever there are heavy trains that routinely operate at speeds under 30 m.p.h. Espee calls them Tractive Effort Booster Units (TEBU), and uses them between matched sets of 7940-series GP40-2s on branchlines in Oregon, Arizona, and Texas.

After thoroughly testing a General Electric set borrowed from the Seaboard Coast Line in 1977, SP commissioned rebuilder Morrison-Knudsen to convert a U25B to a road slug and to provide plans and patterns so that duplicates could be constructed at Sacramento. M-K's #1600, rebuilt from an old Union Pacific high-nose U25B, entered service in May, 1980, simultaneously with twenty EMD GP40-2s (#7940-7959) that were equipped to operate with road slugs.

Sacramento erected thirteen copies, #1601-1613, between April of 1981 and May, 1982. They use frames and trucks from retired U25Bs, along with new electrical cabinets and dynamic brakes. Fuel tanks holding 2800 gallons can transfer fuel to either "mother" unit via hoses. During reconstruc-

tion from U25B specifications, Sacramento added thirty-seven tons of concrete ballast and a one-inch-thick slab of steel for strengthening; the final unit weight is between 271,000 and 280,000 pounds. Unlike most yard slugs (SP's included), the TEBUs can make electrical transition, allowing them to work in road service.

Management considers a GP40-TEBU-GP40 set to be the equivalent of two SD40s or four GP35s, with significant advantages over the former on branchline rails. The two-axle "Blomberg" design has less tendency to derail or cause rail damage than EMD's three-axle Flexicoil, and is favored by SP operating officials for use on those lines which do not have the best in civil engineering. As illustrated here, both Oregon and Arizona branches have put them to use.

New unit train services in Texas are shuttling bulk gravel between a single origin (near Kerrville) and a single destination, (near Houston) moving on just one waybill—with no switching enroute. The gravel trains don't travel very fast, but they need every ounce of tractive effort a TEBU set can exert.

SP decided to buy twenty slug-equipped GP40-2's from EMD and rebuild its own slugs from retired U25B's at Sacramento. The EMD's arrived in April and May of 1980, simultaneously with prototype slug #1600 [rebuilt for SP by Morrison-Knudsen from a UP U25B]. Sacramento was slow in delivery of slugs, so scenes like this at Tenaha, Texas were common: #7946-7949 switch the Santa Fe interchange on November 7, 1980 while awaiting their slug partners. *(John B. Charles)*

SOUTHERN PACIFIC SLUG AND TEBU UNITS, 1973-1986

Numbers	Class	Builder	Converter	Service	Quan.	Delivery
1000-1002	AS600-1	Alco	Ry. Supply	Hump	3	Jul. 73-Aug. 73
1010-1013	ES400-1	EMD	GE, Minneap.	Hump	4	Jun. 79-Aug. 79
1600	GF400LK-1	GE	M-K, Boise	TEBU	1	May 80
1601-1609	GF400R-1	GE	SP, Sacto.	TEBU	9	Apr. 81-Dec. 81
1610-1613	GF400R-1	GE	SP, Sacto.	TEBU	4	Jan. 82-May 82
					21	

NOTES:

1000-1002 Rebuilt from Alco C-628 and C-630 units for use with SD38-2 units at West Colton. Retired in 1985.

1010-1013 Rebuilt by the General Electric Service Shop in Minneapolis from various L&N EMD switchers for use with MP15AC units #2732-2735 at Tucson, Eugene, and Roseville.

1600 Rebuilt from UP U25B #634 as a prototype by Morrison-Knudsen at Boise, Idaho.

1601-1613 Rebuilt from retired SP U25B units by Sacramento Locomotive Works.

The first public indication that Espee was interested in the road slug concept was in the fall of 1977, when General Electric sponsored a visit by this U36B/MATE/U36B set from the Seaboard Coast Line. GE built 20 new road slugs— with EMD trucks—for the SCL. Shown at Sullivan's Curve on Cajon on November 26, 1977 beside a UP train, the trio is proving that it can easily equal a pair of SD40's or a quartet of GP35's. When this picture was taken, the Cutoff had yet to receive CTC. *(Ed Chapman)*

Long a favored photo site, SP's two Arizona main lines cross each other at scenic Cienega Creek a few miles east of Tucson. Passing over the east main are four 6300-series GP35E's, led by TEBU set #7944/1602/7945, in a typical consist for heavy mine-country locals in both Arizona and New Mexico. Most TEBU sets, each with the tractive effort of a pair of SD40's, have found homes on the branches between Tucson and El Paso. *(John C. Lucas)*

Only infrequently are the TEBU's seen alone, as they cannot move by themselves; however, they do carry a supply of fuel, and pumps to deliver it via mu-style hoses to the mother units. The #1612, rebuilt from GE U25B #6758 in 1982, awaits mechanical attention. Below, bracketed by the SD9E's which normally accompany it, TEBU set #7965-1613-7966 lays over. Road slugs have been found useful on Oregon's Toledo and Tillamook Branches, where two-axle trucks are easier on the rail, and have less tendency to derail. Both photos are by Stephen D. Miller at Eugene in June of 1985.

Rock from San Antonio ends up at Galena Park, near Houston, after being delivered by the TEBU sets in unit trains. Needless to say, a very special rate structure makes all this possible—one waybill covers the entire train, and no switching is performed enroute. After unloading at Galena Park, the entire train lays over. The date is October 15, 1982, and TEBU set #7962/1611/7963 is just eight months old.

(Allen Rider)

The Texas TEBU sets are used mainly on unit rock trains; on the point are #7963/1611/7962, all 1982 products of the Sacramento Locomotive Works. Eastbound on the old SA&AP main, known officially as the Bellaire Line, a Galena Park-bound unit rock train crosses the Brazos River at Simonton, Texas. It's 3:15 in the afternoon on Monday, September 12, 1983. This part of the railroad is carded for twenty and 25 m.p.h., a speed range where the TEBU's are most comfortable. Even the high-side hoppers are new, dating from 1981.

(Charles Howard)

Espee put its twenty slug-equipped GP40's into the #7940-7959 series to distinguish them from non-equipped units. Other than internal control modifications, most visible differences are limited to bus bar and fuel line connections on the long hood end. (After buying new #7940-7959 in 1980, SP rebuilt SSW #7600-7607 to GP40E "mothers" #7960-7967 in 1982.) Two complete GP40-2 sets will power the heavy *Clifton Local* on April 25, 1983, but they won't leave until noon.

(John C. Lucas)

The TEBU production line at Sacramento kept rolling into 1982, with one each month being erected in January, February, April, and May. Along with them, Sacramento was turning out eight upgraded GP40's, #7960-7967, rebuilt from Cotton Belt #7600-7607. These were the oldest 645-engined units on the system, dating from the very dawn of their era in January of 1966. Two sets were assigned to Houston, but Sacramento didn't add air conditioners. *(Charles Howard)*

Extra 7953 west, a short *North Line Local,* has just begun its day as it sails through the west switch at Gary, New Mexico on a hot Saturday morning in April of 1983. Standard operating procedure at the time for this assignment required four 6300-series GP35E's augmented by a TEBU set. Nearly five hundred SP EMD's carry cab-top air conditioning as seen here. Ample tractive effort is the order of the day! *(John C. Lucas)*

Far from their normal haunts—but on the way home—#7942-1604-7952 and new GP40-2 #7251 head toward Arizona through Banning, California on May 17, 1985. Most routine maintenance for Arizona-assigned TEBU's is performed at El Paso, but they do wander west on occasion. This is the Valla-Chicago container train, originating in a small, obscure yard near Whittier, which today is running heavy and slow. TEBU's can make electrical transition, so they are relatively fast compared to yard slugs, but their upper limit is still only 28 miles per hour. *(Bruce Veary)*

Once the Lenzen Avenue "Round House" stabled steam in two gauges when San Jose hosted both South Pacific Coast and lessor SP...as pure a shrine on the Sunset Route as can be found. Lurking outside the roundhouse door, however, is CalTrain's Palo Alto, a new Electro-Motive F40PH, with precious little to identify it with Espee tradition. Even the building and tree may not survive the revolution. *(Ted Benson)*

Commute Trains in Transition

Among the very last privately-operated rail commuter operations in the United States, SP's from San Jose to San Francisco was also the only one west of Chicago. Truly the pride of the Railroad, the commute service has been extremely tightly-run; rush hour has to coexist with freight and through passenger service, without any schedule degradation. Freight and switching service is set aside during morning and afternoon rushes; the railroad belongs to commuters during those hours.

However, with two major freeways bracketing the line for its entire 47-mile length, inadequate central-city access, and a gradual loss of jobs in downtown San Francisco, Southern Pacific's commute service has recently fallen upon hard times. Fare increases only drove more customers to their cars or to commuter buses (some of them operated by county governments).

Eventually it became clear that corporate pride would have to be put aside, and the commute operation, if not the tracks themselves, put on the block. Eventually the service was sold to the State of California. Caltrans, the same government agency that builds freeways, took over responsibility for the trains—purchasing all operating services from Southern Pacific.

Initially it appeared that Caltrans would take over SP's existing fleet of cars and locomotives and repaint them; in fact, a small train was redone in new colors. (See page 5 of our 1952-82 *REVIEW* for another picture.) In addition to its photogenic old suburban cars—of which about two dozen were serviceable—SP owned 46 modern gallery cars, built by Pullman-Standard and AC&F between 1955 and 1968.

As it turned out, there was little on the SP roster that was adaptable to push-pull operations (SP never espoused push-pull; as a result their costs for turning trains at terminals were higher than the industry average). Caltrans could have rebuilt the SP gallery cars for push-pull operation, but anticipated problems with heat generated by head-end power conduits.

Furthermore, SP wanted its newer locomotives back for use in freight service. Ten 1967-vintage SDP45 units and three GP40P-2 engines dating from 1974 were the front line of the fleet; if they were removed, Caltrans would be left with only eleven upgraded GP9 units and two SD9's.

The decision was finally reached to buy both new locomotives and new cars. Electro-Motive bid its familiar Amtrak F40PH, modified for push-pull operation. Car bidding was a little more complex, since American carbuilders have all but given up on passenger-car production. The Japanese, using General Electric as subcontractor, were the successful bidders; the cars were assembled from imported shells and domestic subassemblies on Pier 50 in San Francisco.

Early in 1985, the new cars, both cabs and trailers, began appearing in San Francisco. In March of 1985, EMD began shipping the first of eighteen F40PH-2 units. A few brief months of transition were recorded by photographers, but by June, Caltrans was ready to institute full push-pull operation. SP has run its last commute passenger train.

Santa Clara was a definite mix of old and new on June 12, 1985—an hour after San Francisco-bound train #59 left with pushpulls, #42 slid into town with five smoky-shoed suburbans trailing SP 3207—the last run for #42 with ancient equipment. Not that long ago the photographer hated the SDP45's for the Train Masters they turned out to pasture. Now. . . well, now they seemed to be one with the GS 4-8-4's.

(Ted Benson)

Tomorrow and yesterday meet in the middle of "right now" as commute trains #46 and #63 meet at Lenzen Avenue in San Jose on June 4, 1985. New CalTrain F40 #906 leads a mix of subs and SP galleries on outbound train #46; SP "torpedo boat" GP9 #3196 pulls three galleries on #63—while the blend of SP and CalTrain is crowding the distant ready tracks at Lenzen Avenue Roundhouse as well. *(Ted Benson)*

Lined up like modern-day *Sun Tan Specials,* GP40P-2 #3199 and SDP45's #3206 and 3204 wait with their trains in the San Jose coach yard on January 20, 1985, for the end of SUPER BOWL XIX and the return trip to Palo Alto. These trains were part of a fleet of eight operated by Caltrans between San Francisco and Stadium (Palo Alto) for the professional football showdown. *(Jon Pullman Porter)*

Already these scenes are impossible to duplicate! Midday on April 24, 1985 finds newly-arrived interloper #900 comparing noses with SP #3186, 3198, and 3204 at the Seventh Street commute engine terminal in San Francisco. *(Ken Rattenne)* Yesterday and tomorrow...it's twilight time at Lenzen Avenue. Ranks closed against the night, SDP45's #3209 and 3207 (with geep #3197 trailing) huddle close to "torpedo boat" #3195 as the Cal Train F40's pull near...and a pushpull control car trails train 58 into San Jose. On June 12, 1985, SP commute power was taking its final bow. *(Ted Benson)*

Sunset at College Park—46 miles out of One Market Street and nine-tenths of a mile before calling it a day, train 60 storms down the Eastbound Main behind SDP #3207, five subs catching the last light of June 4, 1985, posing a picture about as definitively "SP" as could be found this year; only eight days later, this scene would be erased forever. Do we know that fellow with the tripod, Ted? *(Ted Benson)*

Church nursery kids and parents from San Carlos await an unscheduled stop of commute #53 at Castro (on their way to a picnic) when a strident chime horn on an eastbound commands attention and sends mothers scrambling for young hands. There's no eastbound due here at 2:20 p.m....indeed, this is a media special with CalTrain #916 returning to San Jose on June 12, 1985 ...bringing pushpull service to the Peninsula on Day One.
(Ted Benson)

The Central Coast Chapter of the NRHS (along with the Pacific Coast Chapter of the R&LHS) sponsored two roundtrips as a farewell tribute to SP's arch-roof interurban cars (built 1923-27 as #2085-2159). The third in a quartet of specials operated on that last day passes the abandoned California Canners and Growers cannery (on the right) at Sunnyvale, on June 15, 1985. Eight old cars tag along behind #3207, one of the two SDP45 units SP is planning to save for special passenger train movements in the future.
(Jon Pullman Porter)

After more than a decade without major changes in equipment, both engines and cars on Peninsula commute trains were replaced within a few months by new CalTrain equipment in 1985. Control-cab-equipped #4003 brings up the rear of a southbound commute at Menlo Park on June 14, 1985. This scene illustrates a typical off-peak train in "pull" mode, with only the rear marker lights illuminated.   *(Ken Rattenne)*

Day One for pushpulls in CalTrain commute service finds westbound #59 accelerating through Santa Clara on June 12th at 4:36 p.m. Two smiling enthusiasts have already found the "railfan seat" at the front of control cab #4002 for a first run. The photographer's hopes for conventional SP equipment weren't fulfilled, but no doubt two riders were delighted!   *(Ted Benson)*

SP&SF Numbers	Current SP Numbers	Class	Blt.	Model	Quan.
100-103	1010-1013	ES400G-1	79	Slug	4
301-309	1191-1199	ES409E-1	74	SW900E	9
310-312	1300-1302	ES410E-1	71	NW2E	3
313-323	1304-1314	"	71	"	11
324-327	1316-1319	"	71	"	4
328-332	1320-1324	ES410E-2	72	"	5
333-336	1326-1329	"	72	"	4
338-343	1331, 1333-1337	"	72	"	6
1500-1511	1500-1511	ES615R-1	79	SD7E	12
1512-1542	1512-1542	"	80	"	31
200	1600	GF400LK-1	80	S3-3B	1
201-209	1601-1609	GF400R-1	81	TEBU	9
210-213	1610-1613	"	82	"	4
344-351	2250-2257 (SSW)	ES412C-3	64	SW1200	8
352-353	2258-2259 (SSW)	ES412C-4	64	"	2
354-355	2260-2261 (SSW)	ES412C-4	65	"	2
356-358	2262-2264	ES412-4	64	"	3
359	2266	"	64	"	1
360-364	2267-2271	"	65	"	5
365-371	2272-2278	ES412-5	65	"	7
372-380	2280-2288	"	65	"	9
381-382	2289-2290 (SSW)	ES412C-5	66	"	2
383-384	2292-2293 (SSW)	"	66	"	2
385-386	2294-2295	ES412E-1	72	SW7E	2
387	2296	"	73	"	1
388-391	2297-2300	"	73	SW9E	4
397-398	2301-2302	ES412E-2	73	"	2
402-403	2303-2304	"	73	SW1200E	2
399-400	2305-2306	"	73	SW9E	2
404	2307	"	73	SW1200E	1
401	2308	"	74	SW9E	1
405-407	2309-2311	"	74	SW1200E	3
392-396	2312-2316	ES412E-1	74	"	5
601-613	2450-2462	ES415-1	67	SW1500	13
614-630	2464-2480	"	67	"	17
631-642	2481-2492 (SSW)	ES415C-1	68	"	12
643-660	2493-2510	ES415-2	68	"	18
661-672	2511-2522 (SSW)	ES415C-2	69	"	12
673-690	2523-2540	ES415-3	69	"	18
691-701	2542-2552	"	69	"	11
702-727	2553-2578	"	70	"	26
728-731	2579-2582 (SSW)	ES415C-3	70	"	4
732-739	2583-2590 (SSW)	ES415C-4	71	"	8
740-761	2591-2612	ES415-4	71	"	22
762-828	2613-2679	ES415-5	72	"	67
829-838	2680-2689	ES415-6	73	"	10
900-905	2690-2696	ES415-7	74	MP-15	6
906-911	2697-2701	"	75	"	6
912-932	2702-2722	ES415-8	75	MP15AC	21
933-940	2724-2731	"	75	"	8
965-968	2732-2735	ES415-9	75	"	4
941-964	2736-2759	ES415-8	75	"	24
1700	2877	ES418-7	57	GP9	1
1710, 1711, 1705	2876, 2878-2879	ES418-8	59	"	3
1707, 1706, 1703	2882, 2888-2889	"	59	"	3
1709, 1708	2893-2894	"	59	"	2
1715-1716	2880, 2890	ES418-9	59	"	2
1721, 1731, 1728	2884, 2885, 2887	ES418E-1	70	GP9E	3
1738, 1742	2874, 2892	ES418E-2	71	"	2
1798, 1793	2868, 2870	"	73	"	2
1800, 1797	2898-2899	"	73	"	2
1881	2897	ES418E-3	75	"	1
1902-1903	2873, 2875	ES418R-3	77	"	2
1946	2872	ES418R-4	77	"	1
1583	2961	ES620E-1	76	SD35E	1
1584-1588	2962-2966	ES620R-1	77	"	5
1589-1592	2967-2970	"	78	"	4
1550-1555	2971-2976	ES620-1	73	SD38-2	6
1599	3100	GS425E-1	75	U25BE	1
1580-1582	3102-3103, 3105	ES625E-1	74	SD35E	3
1576-1579	3106-3109	ES625-1	65	SD35	4
1961-1962	3186-3187	EP418E-1	75	GP9E	2
1963-1967	3188-3192	EP418R-1	77	"	5
1968-1969	3193-3194	"	78	"	2
1970-1971	3195-3196	"	79	"	2
4100-4102	3197-3199	EP430-1	74	GP40P-2	3
6500	3200	EF636-1	67	SDP45	1
7900	3201	"	67	"	1
6501-6505	3202-3206	"	67	"	5
7901	3207	"	67	"	1
6506-6507	3208-3209	"	67	"	1
1718-1719	3301, 3303	EF418E-1	70	GP9E	2
1720, 1722-1724	3305, 3307-3309	"	70	"	4
1725-1727	3311-3312, 3314	"	70	"	3
1729-1730	3316-3317	"	70	"	2
1732-1733	3319-3320	"	70	"	2
1734-1735	3322-3323	"	70	"	2
1736-1737	3324-3325	"	71	"	2
1739-1741	3327-3329	EF418E-2	71	"	3
1743-1747	3332-3336	"	71	"	5
1748-1751	3338-3341	"	71	"	4
1752-1755	3342-3345	"	72	"	4
1756-1762	3347-3353	"	72	"	7
1763-1781	3355-3373	"	72	"	19
1782-1788	3374-3380	"	73	"	7
1789-1792	3382-3385	"	73	"	4
1794-1795, 1798	3387-3388, 3392	"	73	"	3
1800-1816	3394-3410	"	74	"	17
1817-1826	3411-3419, 3421	"	75	"	10
1827-1828	3425-3426	"	76	"	2
1829-1831	3428-3430	"	76	"	3
1832-1836	3432-3436	"	76	"	5
1837-1839	3438-3440	EF418R-2	77	"	3
1840	3441	"	79	"	1
1701	3640	EF418-7	57	GP9	1
1702	3648 (SSW)	EF418C-2	59	"	1
1704	3663	EF418-8	59	"	1
1712-1714	3708-3709, 3712	EF418-9	59	"	3
1717	3727	"	59	"	1
1841-1842	3732-3733	EF418E-3	71	GP9E	2
1843-1850	3734-3740, 3742	"	72	"	8
1851-1854	3743-3746	"	73	"	4
1855-1858	3748-3751	"	73	"	4
1859-1863	3753-3757	"	73	"	5
1864-1876	3759-3771	"	74	"	13
1877-1880	3772-3775	"	75	"	4
1882-1885	3777-3780	"	75	"	4
1886-1887	3782-3783	"	75	"	2
1888-1901	3784-3797	"	76	"	14
1904-1908	3800-3804	EF418R-3	77	"	5
1909	3805	"	79	"	1
1910-1913	3808-3811 (SSW)	EF418S-3	75	"	4
1914	3812 (SSW)	"	76	"	1
1915	3813 (SSW)	"	78	"	1
1916-1917	3816-3817	EF418E-4	74	"	2
1918-1919	3818-3819	"	75	"	2
1920-1923	3821-3824	"	75	"	4
1924-1942	3825-3843	"	76	"	19
1943-1945	3844-3846	EF418R-4	77	"	3
1947-1957	3848-3858	"	77	"	11
1958	3859	"	78	"	1
1959	3871 (SSW)	EF418S-4	75	"	1
1960	3873 (SSW)	EF418CR-4	77	"	1
1972	3877	EF418E-5	75	"	1
1973-1974	3878-3879	"	76	"	2
1975-1978	3880, 3882-3884	EF418R-5	77	"	4
1979	3885	"	78	"	1
2795-2797	4060, 4063, 4079	EF420-1	62	GP20	3
2798-2799	4085, 4087	EF420-2	60	"	2
2800	4100	EF420E-1	74	GP20E	1
2801-2803	4102-4104	EF420E-2	75	"	3
2804-2808	4105-4109	"	76	"	5
2809-2816	4111-4118	EF420R-2	77	"	8
2817-2820	4119-4122	"	78	"	4
2821-2822	4124-4125	"	79	"	2
2823-2824	4134, 4137 (SSW)	EF420S-1	74	"	2
2825-2828	4139-4142 (SSW)	EF420S-2	75	"	4
2829-2830	4143-4144 (SSW)	"	76	"	2
2831-2834	4146-4149 (SSW)	EF420CR-2	77	"	4
2835-2838	4150-4153 (SSW)	"	79	"	4
2950	4160	EF420R-3	79	GP35E	1
2951-2954	4200-4203 (SSW)	EF420CR-3	79	GP35E	4
5000-5007	4301-4308	EF618E-1	70	SD9E	8
5008-5018	4310-4320	"	70	"	11
5019-5021	4322-4324	"	70	"	3
5022-5048	4325-4351	"	71	"	27
5049-5053	4352-4356	"	72	"	5
5054-5059	4358-4363	"	72	"	6
5060-5072	4364-4376	"	73	"	13
5073-5083	4377-4387	"	74	"	11
5084-5091	4389-4396	"	74	"	8
5092-5103	4397-4408	"	75	"	12
5104-5114	4409-4419	"	76	"	11
5115-5128	4420-4433	EF618R-1	77	"	14
5129-5133	4434-4438	"	78	"	5
5134-5136	4439-4441	"	80	"	3
5137	4450	EF618E-2	73	"	1
5138	4451	"	74	"	1
2411-2455	4800-4844	EF420-3	80	GP38-2	45

SP&SF Numbers	Current SP Numbers	Class	Blt.	Model	Quan.
3000-3003	5002-5005 (SSW)	EF423C-1	63	GP30	4
3004	5007 (SSW)	"	63	"	1
3005	5009 (SSW)	"	63	"	1
3006-3009	5010-5013	EF423-1	63	"	4
3010-3012	5015-5017	"	63	"	3
8189-8203	5100-5114	GF423-1	80	B23-7	15
5300-5301	5300, 5302	EF623-1	68	SD39	2
5302-5303	5304, 5306	"	68	"	2
5304	5306	"	68	"	1
5305-5307	5308-5310	"	68	"	3
5308-5311	5314-5317	"	68	"	4
5312	5318	EF623-2	70	"	1
3500	6300	EF425R-1	77	GP35E	1
3502, 3504-3508	6303, 6305-6309	EF425K-1	78	"	6
3510, 3512	6311, 6313	"	78	"	2
3519-3520	6320-6321	"	78	"	2
3501, 3503, 3509	6302, 6304, 6310	"	79	"	3
3511, 3513-3518	6312, 6314-6319	"	79	"	7
3521-3522	6322-6323	"	79	"	2
3523-3536	6324-6337	EF425N-1	79	"	14
3537-3543	6338-6344	EF425K-1	79	"	7
3544	6345	EF425N-1	80	"	1
3545-3557	6346-6358	"	79	"	13
3558-3561	6359-6361	EF425K-1	79	"	3
3400-3402	6501-6503 (SSW)	EF425C-1	64	GP35	3
3403-3404	6504, 6505 (SSW)	EF425C-2	64	"	2
3405-3406	6507-6508 (SSW)	"	64	"	2
3407	6511 (SSW)	"	64	"	1
3408-3409	6513-6514 (SSW)	"	65	"	2
3410-3411	6516-6517 (SSW)	"	65	"	2
3412	6519 (SSW)	"	65	"	1
3413-3415	6521-6523	EF425-1	64	"	3
3416-3418	6526-6527, 6533	"	64	"	3
3419-3420	6537-6538	"	64	"	2
3421-3423	6543-6544, 6547	"	64	"	3
3424-3425	6551-6552	"	64	"	2
3426-3428	6554-6556	"	64	"	3
3429-3431	6563-6564, 6566	"	64	"	3
3432-3434	6568, 6570, 6574	"	64	"	3
3435	6576	"	64	"	1
3436-3438	6577, 6579, 6582	EF425-2	64	"	3
3439-3440	6584, 6585	"	64	"	2
3441-3444	6587-6590	"	64	"	4
3445-3446	6593, 6595	"	64	"	2
3447-3448	6597, 6600	EF425-3	64	"	2
3449-3453	6604-6607, 6609	"	64	"	5
3454-3456	6611, 6614-6615	"	65	"	3
3457-3459	6617, 6619-6620	"	65	"	3
3460-3461	6622-6623	"	65	"	2
3462-3464	6628, 6631-6632	EF425-4	65	"	3
3465-3466	6639-6640	"	65	"	2
3467-3471	6643-6646, 6650	"	65	"	5
3472-3473	6652-6653	"	65	"	2
3474-3475	6657-6658	"	65	"	2
3476-3479	6660-6662, 6666	"	65	"	4
3480-3483	6668-6671	"	65	"	4
3484-3486	6674, 6676, 6679	"	65	"	3
3487-3488	6680-6681 (SSW)	EF425C-3	65	"	2
4400-4401	7200-7201	EF435-1	78	GP40X	2
4402-4403	7230-7231	"	78	"	2
4170-4177	7240-7247	EF430-4	84	GP40-2	8
4178-4203	7248-7273 (SSW)	EF430C-3	84	"	26
5501-5544	7300-7343	EF630R-1	80	SD40E	44
5545-5586	7344-7385	"	81	"	42
5500	7399	EF630R-2	81	SD45E	1
6600	7400	EF632R-1	79	SD45E	1
6601-6621	7401-7421	EF632R-2	81	"	21
6622-6664	7422-7464	"	82	"	43
6665-6688	7465-7488	"	83	"	24
6689-6736	7489-7536	"	84	"	48
6737-6760	7537-7560	"	85	"	24
4103-4106	7608-7611	EF430-1	78	GP40-2	4
4107-4121	7613-7627	"	78	"	26
4122-4136	7628-7642 (SSW)	EF430C-2	79	"	15
4137-4138	7644-7645 (SSW)	"	79	"	2
4139-4149	7647-7657 (SSW)	"	79	"	11
4150-4169	7658-7677	EF430-2	80	"	20
8519-8534	7754-7769	GF436-1	84	B36-7	16
8500	7770 (SSW)	GF436C-1	78	"	1
9900	7771	GF436CB-1	78	B36-7B	1
8501-8502	7772-7773 (SSW)	GF436C-1	78	B36-7	2
8342-8407	7774-7799 (SSW)	GF430C-1	80	B30-7	26
8300-8302	7801-7803	GF430-1	78	"	3
8303-8308	7804-7809	GF430-2	78	"	6
8309-8321	7811-7823	"	78	"	13
8322-8381	7824-7883	GF430-3	79	"	60
4000-4016	7940-7956	EF430-3	80	GP40-2	17
4017-4108	7958-7959	"	80	"	2
5910-5979	8230-8299	EF630-11	80	SD40T-2	70
5740, 5742	8300-8301	EF630-3	74	SD40T-2	2
5744-5750 (even)	8303-8306	"	74	"	4
5752-5780 (even)	8307-8321	EF630-5	78	"	15
5782-5790 (even)	8322-8326 (SSW)	EF630C-1	78	"	5
5792-5820 (even)	8327-8341	EF630-9	79	"	15
5741-5753 (odd)	8350-8356	EF630-4	74	"	7
5755-5783 (odd)	8357-8371	EF630-6	78	"	15
5785-5793 (odd)	8372-8376 (SSW)	EF630C-2	78	"	5
5795-5823 (odd)	8377-8391	EF630-10	79	"	15
5825-5834	8489-8498	EF630-7	78	SD40T-2	10
5835-5969	8499-8533	EF630-8	78	"	35
5870-5909	8534-8573	"	79	"	40
	8653, 8662, 8669	GF633-3	70	U33C	3
	8673	"	70	"	1
	8689, 8698	GF633-4	71	"	2
	8703-8705	"	71	"	3
	8712, 8717, 8720	"	71	"	3
	8727	"	72	"	1
	8754, 8756, 8760	GF633-6	72	"	3
	8762	"	72	"	1
	8772-8773	GF633-7	73	"	2
	8776-8777	"	73	"	2
	8780	GF633-8	73	"	1
6300-6301	8818, 8822	EF636-1	66	SD45	2
6302-6304	8859, 8872, 8874	EF636-2	67	"	3
6305-6307	8887, 8889, 8898	"	67	"	3
6308-6310	8900, 8909-8910	"	67	"	3
6311-6313	8925, 8927, 8933	"	67	"	3
6314-6317	8935-8937, 8939	EF636-3	68	"	4
6318-6320	8942, 8944, 8951	"	68	"	3
6321-6323	8953, 8955-8956	"	68	"	3
6324-6328	8958-8962	"	68	"	5
6329-6330	8965, 8968 (SSW)	EF636C-1	68	"	2
6331-6332	8978, 8981 (SSW)	"	68	"	2
6333-6335	8988, 8990, 8992	EF636-4	69	"	3
6336-6338	8993, 8996-8997	"	69	"	3
6339-6341	9000, 9002, 9007	"	69	"	3
6342-6345	9013, 9015-9017	"	69	"	4
6346-6347	9019, 9021	"	69	"	2
6348-6351	9023-9025, 9027	"	69	"	4
6352-6353	9030-9031	"	69	"	2
6354-6356	9034, 9036-9037	"	69	"	3
6357-6360	9040-9042, 9047	"	69	"	4
6361	9049	"	69	"	1
6362-6363	9052, 9055 (SSW)	EF636C-3	69	"	2
6364-6365	9065-9066 (SSW)	EF636C-2	68	"	2
6366	9068 (SSW)	"	68	"	1
6367-6369	9071, 9074-9075	EF636-5	69	"	3
6370-6373	9080-9083	"	69	"	4
6374-6378	9085-9088, 9092	"	69	"	5
6379-6384	9095-9100	"	69	"	6
6385-6386	9104-9105	EF636-6	69	"	2
6387-6390	9107-9110	"	69	"	4
6391-6393	9115-9116, 9120	"	69	"	3
6394	9121	"	69	"	1
6395-6397	9123-9125	"	69	"	3
6398	9127	"	70	"	1
6399	9128	"	69	"	1
6400	9129	"	69	"	1
6401-6403	9130, 9132, 9135	"	70	"	3
6404-6418	9137-9151	"	70	"	15
6419	9155 (SSW)	EF636C-4	70	"	1
7600-7608	9157-9165 (SSW)	EF636C-6	72	SD45T-2	9
7609-7616	9166-9173	EF636-7	72	"	8
7617-7646	9175-9204	"	72	"	30
7647-7650	9206-9209	"	72	"	4
7651-7655	9211-9215	"	72	"	5
7656-7658	9217-9219	"	72	"	3
7659-7678	9221-9240	EF636-8	72	"	20
7679-7698	9241-9260	EF636-9	72	"	20
7699-7719	9261-9281 (SSW)	EF636C-7	73	"	21
7720-7739	9282-9301 (SSW)	EF636C-8	73	"	20
7740-7751	9302-9313	EF636-10	73	"	12
7752	9314	"	74	"	1
7753-7781	9315-9343	EF636-11	74	"	29
7782-7791	9344-9353	EF636-12	75	"	10
7792-7807	9355-9370	"	75	"	16
7808-7815	9371-9378 (SSW)	EF636C-9	75	"	8
7816-7839	9380-9404 (SSW)	"	75	"	25

Late afternoon on the Brightside Curve in Niles Canyon finds the East Pleasanton Turn snarling uphill from the Bay with SW-1500's #2626 and 2674 on the head end. Espee's Niles Canyon rails were in their hundred-fifteenth summer this May 29, 1984...the last summer they would see revenue service. It has been proposed that the Pacific Locomotive Association operate these rails as a steam museum sometime in the future.

(Ted Benson)

The SP/SSW Roster in Pictures

A roster of Southern Pacific and Cotton Belt diesels is presented here in a "snapshot" dated the fall of 1985. On the previous two pages appears a tabulation of locomotives owned by the combined roads, along with their current class, year built, model number, and quantity in service. The following forty-eight pages illustrate each model on the 1985 SP/SSW roster, either with static locomotive portraits or views of examples of that model in action.

The author was privileged to participate in the initial steps taken toward a post-merger locomotive renumbering plan, a portion of which is included on the two previous pages. However, as of this writing, the SP&SF merger has not been approved, and future locomotive numbering remains tentative. Specific old-to-new number correlations will not be made until the eve of the merger, so that last-minute retirements will have minimal effect on the final plan. As presently arranged, the renumbering plan has SP and Santa Fe blocks abutting each other; a retirement causes all higher numbers in that class to decrease by one.

It should be pointed out also that many units are shown with SP&SF numbers that may never be physically applied to the locomotives. SP's smaller and older switchers are presently in dead storage and may never run again; the numbers reserved for them may only show up on paper. In short, until the combined roster is "fixed" by corporate edict, nothing is guaranteed.

No SP&SF numbers are shown for the General Electric U33C fleet, delivered between 1969 and 1974, because virtually all of them are out of service—and no upgrade/scrap decision for them has been reached yet. Without counting them, only about seven per cent of the current roster was constructed by General Electric!

The author's list of locomotives upgraded since 1970 now fills more than twenty pages. If you would like a copy, please send $2, care of Shade Tree Books.

It seems that something always slips through the cracks...the roster on page 83 was typeset without listing fourteen GE U33C units:

8585-8586	GF633-10	74	U33C	2
8588-8597	"	74	"	10
8598-8599	"	75	"	2

Faithfully leading off our Picture Roster for its final bow, hump slug #1001 is pictured at its home in West Colton in August of 1977. In 1984, time caught up with the three Alco Century rebuilds, and they were sent to Los Angeles for a general overhaul. Once there, it became clear that they would never return to service, if for no other reason than crew complaints over their vertical step arrangement. A career of eleven years has been completed. *(Duane Karam)*

One of the two yard slug sets operating at Tucson Yard is MP15AC #2733 and slug #1012, the latter rebuilt from a Louisville & Nashville EMD switcher by the General Electric Service Shop in Minneapolis. Two additional sets are assigned to Roseville; yardmasters give them low marks because of their slow operating speed. A summer thunderstorm coincides with afternoon break on August 12, 1984.

(James R. Doughty)

Tucked away in the heart of the San Joaquin Valley is little-seen and scarcely-documented Visalia Electric...a prime candidate for annihilation come merger day. In a scene straight out of the Pacific Electric picturebook, SW900E #1197 takes an empty PFE reefer over the Kaweah River above Lemon Cove, eastbound for Sequoia on March 29, 1985.

(Ted Benson)

Not many Southern Pacific diesels remain in service that can trace their history back into the forties. Upgraded NW2 #1306 began its service as Texas & New Orleans #87 back in August of 1949, becoming #1929 in the general renumbering of 1965. Then in May of 1971 it was run through the Houston Shops, where it was completely renewed as #1306. Exactly nine years later, #1306 rests near the Amtrak station in Houston.

(David M. Bernstein)

East Yokohl, California, rates no mention in Uncle Sam's list of Post Offices—but it is a valid station name on the timetable of subsidiary Visalia Electric, northeast of Exeter on the little-used line to Lemon Cove. On June 1, 1984, SW900 #1196 was on its way through this metropolis with seven empty hoppers for gravel loading. Relatively little of the area's citrus moves by rail anymore; gravel accounts for most outbound carloadings.

(John Ford)

The *Clark Local* services industrial spurs to the east of Sparks (Reno) Nevada, picking up and making setouts as necessary. Pictured on the Local at the town of Clark—eighteen miles from its point of origin—on May 13, 1981, is SD7E #1533, about a year after being remanufactured at Sacramento from SD7 #1428. It was built in 1953 as #5321, so it has had a long, productive service career.   *(Ken Rattenne)*

Los Angeles-maintained SD7E's #1506 and 1501 were far from home at Tucumcari, New Mexico, on April 10, 1982; their services were needed in Kansas City. This particular unit was built as #5332 back in 1953, and was upgraded in Sacramento in August of 1979. The SD7E's will retain their 1500-series numbers on the SP&SF roster.   *(Samuel L. Gonzales)*

The suburb of Walnut, seven miles west of Pomona, is a favored vantage point for SP photos, as it still retains a bit of rural character amid urban sprawl—and even boasts a hill or two! At Walnut on March 22, 1981, is a typical Los Angeles-West Colton "shuttle," delivering assorted loads and empties for classification. The power today is made up of what would normally be considered switchers: five SD7E's and a lone SW-1500. The units are: #1512, 2616, 1506, 1507, 1513, and 1516.   *(John E. Shaw)*

Sporting closely-spaced stacks resulting from an exhaust manifold reversal, upgraded SW9 #2301 awaits its next call in September of 1978 at the yard office in Avondale, Louisiana (across the Mississippi from New Orleans). As with the NW2E's, most of this class is presently in dead storage at Hardy Street in Houston.

(John B. Charles)

At the south end of Bayshore Yard, four switchers have worked their way down from Seventh Street in San Francisco for a maintenance stop on July 10, 1976. The dispatcher has brought them the long way—completely past the yard itself—before letting them in on one of the leads. Two SW-1200 and two NW2E units make up the group: #2262, 2267, 1312, and 1335.

(Rodney Ciganovich)

One of those occasions when the photographer was thankful he had a camera came about at Niles, California, on September 8, 1982, a day when Southern Pacific was moving thirteen (count 'em!) dead switchers from Bayshore to West Oakland for storage at Desert Yard. For the record, the units were: #2267, 2283, 2266, 2280, 2281, 1335, 1198, 1194, 1199, 1193, 1329, 1195, and 1309. SW-1200 #2284 provided the power.

(Don Buchholz)

Yes, trains do run through posh Beverly Hills—or at least they did until recently. A few carload rail customers in this predominantly retail, office, and residential neighborhood required SP to retain this trackage until the mid-eighties, when it was finally abandoned. SW-1500 #2471 is leaving Beverly Hills, passing Century City on the West Los Angeles Branch, on May 9, 1976. *(Gary G. Allen)*

Mission Bay Yard in San Francisco was once home for a half-dozen switchers; now it is but a ghost of its former self, but SP wants to redevelop this choice land as offices and condos. Class ES415-4 SW-1500 #2598 is all alone, almost in the shadow of skyscrapers. *(Ken Rattenne)* Below, the camera of the late Richard A. Smith brings us this study of a local returning from the Simi Valley through Chatsworth on March 17, 1977. This SW-1500 is from an order for sixty-seven units, #2613-2679, delivered in 1972. SP&SF presently plans to renumber the SW-1500's as #601-837.

An earlier page in this book has a Baldwin-Lima-Hamilton S-12 holding down the assignment at Weed, California—but Baldwins no longer roam the rails of the Espee. In their place is an impressive fleet of 239 SW-1500 units, purchased between 1967 and 1973. An overcast September 24, 1981 eliminates the usual shadows beneath this 1971-vintage SW-1500, highlighting its Flexicoil trucks and 1100-gallon fuel tank.
(Don Bain)

Using virtually the same superstructure and identical power transmission as the SW-1500, Electro-Motive came up with the MP-15. Its longer frame accommodates road trucks and a larger, 1300-gallon fuel tank. Arrival of twelve of these in the Bay Area in 1975 allowed SP to transfer or retire the last of its Fairbanks-Morse switchers. The picture was taken by the author at Pittsburg on February 19, 1976.

The final permutation of EMD's 1500-hp switcher is this MP15AC, which uses an alternator to generate traction power, and features a "tunnel motor" radiator and 1500 gallons of fuel. Fifty-eight, #2702-2759, were delivered in August and September of 1975. Leased to the Cotton Belt almost since delivery, #2716 poses at the SSW yard in Tyler, Texas, on May 17, 1978. SP was the last large railroad to buy switchers in any quantity, and hasn't asked for quotes in a decade; observers predict that the market for new switchers is dead. *(John B. Charles)*

Not all the engines pictured in this section have survived; GP9 switcher #2891 was sold in May of 1985 to the Chrome Locomotive Company. In December of 1979, however, it was on active duty a few miles from Disneyland at SP's Anaheim facility. This is the former #3717, one of the factory low-nose GP9's, that was never upgraded. The incongruous pilot plow won't be needed in Orange County! *(Bryan Griebenow)*

A gathering of SP/SSW locomotives almost inconceivable to Californians is routine at Avondale Yard, across the Mississippi from New Orleans. MP15AC's #2710 and 2704 just tied up on this gloomy after-noon in December of 1982. The big EMD switchers replaced Alco Centuries on transfer runs across the Huey Long Bridge; this series is expected to become SP&SF #912- 964 after the merger. On the right is GP35E #4200, followed by GP20E's #4153, 4145, and 4152, all about ready to leave. *(David C. Lustig)*

The scenic highlight of today's Santa Cruz Branch is this bridge over Soquel Creek at Capitola, immor-talized in pictures since narrow gauge days on the Santa Cruz Railroad. (See MacGregor's *South Pacific Coast,* page 246, for the definitive vintage photo.) The identical vantage point on January 2, 1985 yielded this view of the local with SP #2890, SSW #3813, and SP #3313 on their way from Watsonville Junction. *(Jon Pullman Porter)*

As gleaming blue Missouri Pacific EMD's are ignominiously dragged backward into a Houston Belt & Terminal Yard, begrimed SP SD35E units propel another cut of cars over the crest of Englewood Yard's double-track hump. The twenty-nine SD35's were built in 1964-65 as #4816-4844, becoming #6900-6928 in the renumbering. All that remain are in the 2961 and 3102 series, assigned to heavy switching chores here and in California.   *(Joseph A. Strapac)*

Since these pictures in June of 1983, #2961-2969 have received new paint, although they are still on duty at Englewood Yard, SP's sprawling facility on the east side of Houston. After the merger, this yard will absorb Santa Fe's present local activities, while the SD35E's will become SP&SF #1582-1591 if present renumbering plans are carried out; the SD35E's will then be carrying their fifth numbers!   *(Joseph A. Strapac)*

Hump slug "mothers" #2971-2976, SD38-2's built for West Colton Yard service in 1973, came from the factory without SP's usual "light show" arrangements at either end. When operating as in this picture (taken in March of 1979) the slug generates traction only at three axles; the rear truck has no power. Seven years later, the slugs were set aside and replaced with SD7 or SW-1500 units spliced between the SD38's.   *(David C. Lustig)*

In a grand experiment that was just too costly to succeed, SP tried to upgrade two U25B's to more modern specifications. Look closely—that's a completely new and rearranged hood back to the radiators, with equal-height doors and removable roof hatches; the undercab doors are all larger, too. Completed in 1975, it was demoted to switching/shuttle assignments by 1980 when photographed at City of Industry, east of Los Angeles. *(Mark A. Denis)*

SD35's #3106-3109 are all West Colton switchers, called to work here when the Alco Centuries were retired. None of the four has been through an upgrading; this is the former #6928 in fresh paint and a new number at its home yard on the first day of summer in 1980. These 2500-hp. units simply cannot deliver enough horsepower per axle to be effective any longer in road service, so they will spend the rest of their days as switchers. *(Mark A. Denis)*

Orange county doesn't generate many outbound carloadings anymore; it's mainly a consuming neighborhood. SP's service to numerous rail customers is provided by the *Anaheim Hauler*, presently originating at City of Industry. On November 19, 1983, this train was returning home through Buena Park with SD35E #3102 and SD39 #5322, a typical combination. Incidentally, those illuminated classification lights are history now; SP is removing them from locomotives. *(John Totten)*

"Torpedo Boat" #3196 was the last commute GP9 to be upgraded, emerging from Sacramento on February 8, 1979. A few weeks later, on April 13, it powered San Jose-bound train #118 at Millbrae. SP has four of these geeps without dynamic brake blisters (although none of the commute GP9's have working dynamic brakes). In 1985, all eleven commute GP9's finally lost their jobs to new CalTrans F40PH units. *(Gordon Lloyd, Jr.)*

A one-of-a-kind train helps CALTRANS show its colors while waiting for new equipment to arrive. Northbound #57 is about to make its first scheduled stop, at College Park, carded for 3:38 p.m., on November 14, 1984. The only leased SP GP9E to be repainted, #3187, is in charge, along with all three of the SP gallery cars thus far redone in new colors. Since the spring of 1985, #3187 has had an uncertain future. *(Ken Rattenne)*

The newest stop on the SP/CalTrans commute is the station of Lawrence in the heart of Silicon Valley, catering to the "reverse commuter" whose home is further north on the Peninsula. SP #3195 has just discharged a passenger load of engineers, programmers, and hi-tech executives from the north, while a Santa Clara County Transit bus waits for the riders to board for delivery to companies such as Lockheed and National Semiconductor. *(Ken Rattenne)*

The first passenger train in thirty years on Oregon's Coos Bay Branch was headed by GP40P-2's #3199 and 3197 on May 20, 1983. Four leading cars were from SP's "Phantom Fleet" of passenger equipment, followed by two leased Sierra Western coaches and a lounge in Northern Pacific colors, followed in turn by two SP business cars. The line's principal business provides a backdrop for the locomotives: that's a mountain of wood chips.

(Ed Collar, Jr.)

Over the years, locomotive axle loadings have edged upward; F7's of the fifties rarely carried more than thirty tons per axle. However, GP40P-2 #3198 weighs in at an impressive 280,900 pounds, or thirty-five tons per axle. Of course, every option imaginable, including a steam generator and air conditioning, contributes to its obesity. On weekend freight duty, #3198 was photographed at Roseville on March 18, 1978. They will become full-time freight units #4100-4102 on the SP&SF.

(Duane Karam)

It's difficult to realize that the ten SDP45's, delivered in the spring of 1967 to relieve Alco PA-2's on the City of San Francisco, are now eighteen years old and currently out of work themselves. Replaced in their recent commute role, they are to be revised to full-freight service by conversion of their water tanks to fuel. The SP&SF will probably keep two in reserve passenger assignments for special trains. This picture dates from April of 1975 at Bayshore, when the SDP's had just taken over for the Train Masters.

(Vic Reyna:McGuffin collection)

Southern Pacific/CalTrans train #46 speeds southbound toward its San Jose destination (where it's due to arrive at 6:03 p.m.), near the roundhouse and service tracks on the last lap of its run from San Francisco on June 25, 1982, long before plans had jelled for new diesels and push-pull cars as seen elsewhere in this book. If present plans work out, SP #3201 and 3207 will be retained for special passenger duties as SP&SF #7900 and 7901. *(Ken Rattenne)*

Relieved of commute duties for the weekend, five SDP45's take tonnage over the Hill to Sparks on a Saturday afternoon in August of 1981; tomorrow they'll make the return trip and be back in San Jose in time for the rush hour on Monday. This is the #2 (eastbound) track at Shed 47—past the summit at Norden, where the descending grade is 1.6%. *(Clint Nestell)*

This class EF418-8 GP9 is one of the few which did not receive an upgrading at Sacramento, so it still carries the number assigned in 1965. It was built in March of 1959 as #5800, and is expected to become SP&SF #1704 after the merger (unrebuilt GP9's will be numbered according to their ages). It is pictured at Los Angeles on December 8, 1979. *(Dick Stephenson)*

The very last of hundreds of upgraded GP9E units to emerge from Sacramento was #3886, which entered service on March 9, 1979. Two years later, it was awaiting servicing at West Colton Yard. The only common carrier GP9's built by EMD with a low short hood were SP #5872-5891, delivered in August and September of 1959. They became #3708-3727 in the 1965 renumbering; ten were upgraded as #3877-3886. The #3886 was later wrecked, and is now the property of a locomotive dealer. *(Joseph A. Strapac)*

The *Fontana Local* was led by three typical GP9E units from the Los Angeles Freight Pool on Washington's Birthday, 1981. In addition to leading #3320, 3346 and 3438 help handle this heavy train. Since this picture was taken, the Kaiser Steel mill in Fontana has closed down. *(Paul Wester)*

California's San Joaquin and Sacramento Valleys have been a racetrack for countless GP9's since the mid-fifties. At right, GP9E #3348 pauses at Mendota with the West Side Hauler on July 28, 1984. The classic Southern Pacific station architecture is enhanced by the Valley's last train order signal mast (although few trains pick up their orders on the fly here anymore). Since this picture, the West Valley line has been converted to Direct Traffic Control, with movement orders transmitted by radio. *(John Ford)* Below, a superb example of paced photography freezes fast-moving #3435 in mid-stride on an afternoon in January of 1979. This particular locomotive had been upgraded at Houston in June, 1976.

(David Styffe)

The San Joaquin Valley town of Sanger sees only three trains per week, all of them at regularly irregular times. In the winter of 1983, the *Ivanhoe Locals* appeared "sometime" on Tuesdays, Thursdays, and Saturdays. The Saturday trip was predictably short, for the crew had "life or death" college football waiting at home!
(*John Ford*)

Although human tourists throng Santa Cruz, locomotive tourists have only visited once (the SCL MATE set). The daily task of the *Santa Cruz Local* is mostly left to GP9E and SD9E workers, as can be seen in this September 24, 1984, view of GP9E #3403 and four units making their careful way to the Santa Cruz Yard before going up the Davenport Branch.
(*Ken Rattenne*)

Somewhere east of Lodi, in central California, GP9E #3882 and three compatriots are delivering coal to fuel the kilns of Calaveras Portland Cement Company at Valley Springs. The train is crossing California Highway #12, which follows the Kentucky House Branch into the oak-studded foothills. In February of 1981, the branch was still busy; since then it has become a storage spur for out-of-service equipment. The cement plant is presently closed down.

(Tom Taylor)

A relic of Electro-Motive's earliest production of turbocharged diesels is Cotton Belt GP20E #4149, photographed by the author at Beaumont, Texas, in June of 1983. Originally built in December of 1961 as SSW #810, this unit became #4040 in the renumbering. In November of 1977, it was given a new 2,000-horsepower 16-645 engine (without turbocharger) to replace its original, troublesome turbocharged 567. It now has two exhaust stacks, and is essentially the equivalent of a GP38-2.

Reluctant darlings of the number collectors are the five GP35's upgraded in 1979 and fitted with 2,000-horsepower 16-645 engines like most of the GP20E's. They are numbered SP #4160 and SSW #4200-4203, and are infrequently seen or photographed west of Houston. Wired up to the SEARCH locomotive tester at Houston Shops in November of 1981, #4203 (formerly Cotton Belt #6515) is almost lost among all the cables. *(John B. Charles)*

An unrebuilt GP20 on the point on Coast Line freight in 1985 is an occasion for raised eyebrows, but—despite diminished business—Southern Pacific is currently short on serviceable power. Both borrowed power and third-string locomotives have shown up in unlikely locations, as testified by #4079 and 5300 leading a short San Luis Obispo-Oxnard turn on January 18, 1985 along the beach above Ventura between Dulah and Seacliff. *(Bruce Veary)*

Considering the amount of sophisticated engineering that went into them, the five non-turbocharged GP35E's have everything SP could ask for on a GP38-2 (although they carry 2,600 gallons of fuel to 3,600 on the GP38-2, with its longer frame). A proposal has been made to re-engine more GP35's with 12-710 prime movers, but this idea appears premature in light of the merger; consider the 4160/4200 series a dead end. *(John B. Charles)*

Many SD9E units assigned to Roseville carry foldaway icicle-breaker "antlers" on their cab roofs, and a few have been fitted with this spinner windshield, that flicks snow and ice away from the engineer's line of view. These reliable machines were delivered between 1954 and 1957, undergoing upgradings between 1970 and 1980. It is expected that they will become SP&SF #5000-5128.
(Mark A. Denis)

"Power-hungry Amtrak leases SP SD9's?" Well, not really. What is actually happening here is that SP #4311 is waiting for the westbound *California Zephyr* at Sparks on January 22, 1984 so that it can attach four "Reno" Superliner coaches to the rear of the train for tired gamblers to ride back to Sacramento and the Bay Area.
(Ken Rattenne)

A pair of SD9's is in charge of the *Oil Cans* at Stege, between Albany and Richmond on San Francisco Bay. This is one of SP's senior unit train services, bringing crude oil from Utah for refining in the Bay Area. At this point, the train is empty and is just getting underway on its return journey. *(Don Buchholz)*

SD9E's #4430 and 4421 wait with the westbound Portland Division Relief Outfit (wrecker) south of Albany Yard on June 17, 1985, to complete a meet before going on to clean up a derailment. Derrick #7180 is still steam-powered, and carries a turbogenerator on the roof to power its myriad of spot and floodlights.

(Stephen D. Miller)

A trio of upgraded SD9's takes the eastbound empties of the *East Pleasanton Turn* up Niles Canyon at Farwell in August of 1980. About the only thing in this picture older than the 1896 bridge over Alameda Creek is the canyon itself! This train's reason for being is rock and aggregate tonnage generated in the Livermore Valley and distributed from Redwood City; often it acts just like a "real" unit train.

(Ted Benson)

Cadillacs at work....at the upper left are three leading the westbound *Tracy Drag* through Madera on June 27, 1982 in a photo by Ken Rattenne. On the right are three more, struggling with a trainload of lumber and forest products on what has always been their home turf, the Northwestern Pacific, on April 15, 1982. *(Bruce Evans)* Below, another traditional venue for SD9E's has been Oregon branchlines. The westbound *McMinnville Turn* clatters over Villa Road trestle as it enters Newberg, Oregon, in March of 1982.

(Don Buchholz)

Forty-five miles east of San Antonio, eastbound extra 4805 has taken the siding at Kingsbury, Texas. On the point are 1980-built GP38-2's #4805-4806, on a rare outing in 1981 when most of this class of 45 units was stored under wraps, awaiting an upturn in business. This is EMD's "GP9 for the eighties," with a normally-aspirated 645 engine of 2000 horsepower. Hearing these (or the SD38-2's) is like taking a trip back in time! *(John B. Charles)*

Forty-five GP38-2 units, #4800-4844, were constructed on the eve of the recession in 1980, and in consequence have spent many months in storage. (See our *Southern Pacific Review 1981*, page 52.) One of the few to escape made a brief visit to Northern California for fuel-economy testing. Here's #4800 at Antelope Yard, Roseville, on May 3, 1981—when all local cameras were gathered at a museum opening at Sacramento, a few miles to the southwest. *(Mark A. Denis)*

Relatively few GP38-2's have yet migrated to California; most are maintained at Houston for branchline duties in Texas. However, they have been tested in snow-fighting work; #4843 carries foldaway icicle-breaker "antlers" for clearing snowsheds. A hot evening at Exeter in September of 1984 finds it, however, at Richgrove on the Exeter Branch—far from any snow—in the hole for a meet with the Santa Fe *819 Train*, which has trackage rights here. *(John Ford)*

The San Diego & Arizona Eastern was built on a tight budget and never generated enough business to warrant a substantial track upgrading, so the largest power used there was typically GP30 and GP35 units. GP30 #5012 and GP9E #3762 have come in to San Diego on the night freight in April of 1976, and will leave again tonight. Meanwhile, they lay over at the SD&AE "barn" south of downtown in the company of switchers. Even before taking on a light-rail tenant in the form of the San Diego Trolley, the SD&AE was most active at night. *(Bob Lehmuth:McGuffin collection)*

Above, early in 1982, GP38-2 #4800 and B23-7 #5101 were brought together for fuel consumption comparisons; here they sandwich instrument car #252 at Houston on January 25, 1982. The fifteen GE B23-7's (#5100-5114) will be combined with Santa Fe's as SP&SF #8189-8203 after the merger. *(Stuart Schroeder)* Below, extra 5103 west handles the last leg of van train *LADAT* from Ennis to Dallas near Garrett on October 27, 1984. In these days of 3600-horsepower B-B's, these 1980-vintage, 2300-horsepower machines would be expected on branchlines instead of leading mainline freights. *(Ed Chapman)*

A locomotive design which hasn't found much favor outside the SP and a few others is the SD39, which utilizes a turbocharged V12 (the same basic "block" as in SW-1500's) to generate 2300 horsepower. Long a favorite around Southern California, SP's #5300-5325 have drawn grueling chores since built in 1968 and 1970, as evidenced by begrimed #5324 at Bakersfield in May of 1974. In 1985, #5319-5325 sit idle at Sacramento, their leases expired. *(Joseph A. Strapac)*

As far as we know, no one motorcades SD39's! This is just normal afternoon traffic on the Santa Ana Freeway at Euclid Avenue in Anaheim on February 19, 1983. The *Anaheim Hauler* waits to enter the small yard area with today's loads, for distribution tomorrow by switchers to various customers out on lesser branches. SP rails parallel Interstate #5 all the way into Santa Ana. *(John Totten)*

Extra 6332 east, the *Douglas Local,* **heads east just before sunset on April 22, 1983 at Cienega, Arizona, with but one empty hopper and a Cotton Belt bay-window caboose. Four GP35E's, including #6332, 6319, and 6329, provide the power. This location, now called Empire, is located at milepost 1007.4 on trackage originally installed by the El Paso & Southwestern and acquired by the SP in 1924.** *(John C. Lucas)*

A quartet of GP35E's bracket a GP40-2/TEBU set in the siding at Lordsburg, New Mexico, in May of 1984 as an eastbound freight disappears into a distant mirage. Built for the ages, Lordsburg's monumental coaling tower would cost more to demolish than it could bring as scrap, so this relic of steam days—unused since 1950—still stands as a landmark. *(Robert R. Harmen)*

The official "home turf" for the 6300-series GP35E's (upgraded in-kind with turbocharged 567 engines by contractors Morrison-Knudsen and Canadian National) is between Tucson and El Paso, where they have been assigned since 1979. A crowded Lordsburg "Yard" is switched in May of 1984 by #6324 and a TEBU set prior to leaving town with a fresh crew. This unit was formerly #6678, upgraded by CN in January of 1979 when SP ran short on locomotives and space to repair them. *(Ken Rattenne)*

Aha! What have we here, but a matched set of four GP35E's, rare in Southern California, leading a Phoenix-bound drag past West Palm Springs at 3:25 p.m. on October 2, 1982. The engines are #6342, 6322, 6305, and 6355, all stencilled for their home port of Tucson. SP&SF intends to put the GP35E rebuilds in its 3500-3560 series. *(Bruce Veary)*

In contrast to the relatively far-flung activities of GP35E's in the 6300 series, non-upgraded GP35 units in the 6500's and 6600's are becoming rare. They were cantankerous when first delivered, and never quite lived up to their performance potential. The #6531 joins L&N #3020 and B30-7 #7873 on the *Hearne-Yoakum Local* in switching moves at Giddings, Texas on August 16, 1979. In September of 1984, #6531 met its fate as a trade for a new GP40-2, when it was scrapped at LaGrange. *(Joe McMillan)*

Gradually making their way over most mainline rail mileage in the United States are Department of Transportation test cars #T3 and T4. Back in April of 1979, they were photographed in the pine forests of East Texas, a few miles north of Cleveland, on Espee's Houston-to-Shreveport line, in the company of GP35 #6540. This GP35 was one of eight sent back to their builder in 1984 as tradein credit on new units. Remaining unrebuilt GP35 units are scheduled to become SP&SF #3400-3488. *(Chris Raught)*

Already confined to Portland Division shuttle service, Sulzers #7032 and 7031 ease around one of the tightest mainline curves on the SP, across the Willamette River at Portland Union Station (East Portland). The date is Sptember 11, 1981, and ninety-five cars stretch out behind the drawbar. Before long, the red-and-orange 2800-horsepower units will be put away in storage. *(Don Buchholz)*

Gleaming orange "Daylight" Sulzer units graced our 1978-79 cover, but now they sit retired in Eugene, as pictured on June 15, 1985. Arguably the most successful of all Morrison-Knudsen's re-enginings with the Swiss prime mover, the SP's four V12-equipped TE70-4s units were finally undone by their complex German-import cooling systems, which kept them in the shop more than out on the road. *(Stephen D. Miller)*

A little out of place at the Roseville Yard in May of 1981, 3500- horsepower GP40X #7231 is more often found in Southern California. SP bought four of these semi-demonstrators in 1978, two Locotrol radio masters and two remotes, but almost never uses the in "radio" mode. Santa Fe's otherwise- similar GP40X units are fitted with more conventional trucks instead of this design, which was supposed to reduce weight transfer and wheelslip. Significantly, subsequent orders have all reverted to the classic "Blomberg" design. *(Mark A. Denis)*

113

Extra 7201 west accelerates past the caboose of a waiting eastbound at Covell, on the Valley mainline. GP40X units #7201 and 7230 have 133 cars in tow, and make the meet as fast as the ctc dispatcher can put out signals. Covell siding, 23 miles south of Stockton and five miles north of Modesto, was created by installation of ctc in 1963.

(Ted Benson)

Three quarters of SP's GP40X fleet has an eastbound (geographically southbound) freight behind the drawbar south of San Luis Obispo on August 9, 1981. At work on extra 7200 east are #7200, 7230, 7231, and SD45T-2 #9158. Once their "elephant ears" were removed, the GP40X's were routinely confined to Los Angeles-Bay Area duties for many years.

(John E. Shaw)

It's certainly a long way from the California Coast to Wootton, Colorado, but this combination of stiff grades, high altitude, and power consist are just too interesting to pass up. The date is November 3, 1979, and #7201 is demonstrating for its builder on the Santa Fe at Raton Pass. Electro-Motive has brought along its whole menagerie of test units to help wring out the GP40X concept and prepare for advent of the production-model GP50. *(Ray Kenley)*

When it was announced that Southern Pacific was to become one of the corporate sponsors for the 1984 Olympics, employees at the Los Angeles Locomotive Plant hatched the idea of painting a locomotive to honor the occasion...hence this result, painted in great secrecy at the roundhouse in early May of 1984. SD40E #7347 was upgraded from #8479 in January of 1981; early in 1985 it reverted to grey colors. In August, it was destroyed in a collision on the Burlington Northern. *(Dick Stephenson)*

When the New Orleans Daylight was returning to Southern California in June of 1984, Southern Pacific was ready to supply helpers for Beaumont Hill in two different special paint schemes. SD40E's #7342 and 7347 wait at West Colton to depart for Twentynine Palms to assist the inbound steam special on June 17, 1984. A near-twin to the #7342 appears in color on the back cover of our 1981 *REVIEW.* *(Joe Shine)*

115

Uppper left: extra 7456 west waits to enter Englewood Yard in Houston in June of 1983, with an SD45E on the point, followed by two of Southern's high-nose SD45's. *(Joseph A. Strapac)* Upper right: Between Newhall Tunnel and Sylmar on October 17, 1982, SD40E #7355 led four other six-motor units on the southbound *BRLAT* with vans for Los Angeles from the Pacific Northwest. *(Bruce Veary)* Below, another van train, from Los Angeles to Memphis, crosses the Harahan Bridge over the Mississippi into its destination city in August of 1981 with SD40E #7364 in charge.

(Dave Johnston)

Thirty hoppers of Utah coal obediently trail #7360/8703/3778 eastbound through Hayward, California on November 28, 1981; behind them are eighty more cars of mixed freight. SD40E #7360 was upgraded in March of 1981 from SD40 #8472, and is expected to become #5561 in the planned SP&SF renumbering. No future is planned for the U33C. *(Don Buchholz)*

A fast Eugene-to-Los Angeles freight pauses briefly at Oxnard in October of 1984 with two new SD45E's on the point: #7500 and 7511. The lead engine was upgraded the previous April from #8921, while #7511 followed on June 28th, having been rebuilt from #8901. Sacramento is upgrading two dozen in 1985, #7537-7560, and has already began to choose candidates for 1986 work—although those units will probably come out as SP&SF 6700's. *(Bruce Veary)*

Running as scheduled #46, extra 7514 east is at Seger, Texas, on October 31, 1984. Trains run "backward" between Corsicana and Hearne in deference to a tradition going back to the Houston & Texas Central. At Hearne, #46 will become westbound #45 for the remainder of its trip to Los Angeles. The SD45E had only been in service since July of 1984, having been upgraded from old #8926. *(Ed Chapman)*

Where once Southern Pacific engines were exchanged for those of the Rock Island, now a minor formality puts SP trains in the hands of the Cotton Belt. Overlooking the station at Tucumcari, New Mexico on April 11, 1982, we see SP SD40E #7326 and Cotton Belt GP40-2 #7634 accelerate out of twn. One less formality was necessary after October 1, 1985: on that date both the SP and SSW finally began using the same rulebook!

(Samuel L. Gonzales)

It looks like the mountains of Mars, but in reality it is a light on the CTC machine labelled "Kinter," some eighteen miles east of Yuma in Arizona's Gila River Valley. Cotton Belt GP40-2 #7649, built in January of 1979, leads a quintet westbound with auto racks in the early morning light of January 8, 1984. These late-model 40's will become red-and-yellow SP&SF 4100's if present plans are carried through.

(John Totten)

In a scene designed to gladden a locomotive salesman's heart, here are nine units on the *KCLAY* approaching Corona, New Mexico (fifty miles northwest of Carrizozo, at an elevation of 6600 feet) on August 5, 1981. Today, this hot merchandiser has been given #7669, 8827, 9135, 7340, 9344, 8596, 9310, 6346, and 6307!

(John Lucas)

Herein lies a tale...extra 7616 east, with over 100 cars in tow behind four GP40-2's, couldn't make the hill between San Simon, Arizona and Steins, New Mexico—and stalled on the state line. The dispatcher had the crew of westbound *CHLAT* tie down their train at Steins and lend three units to tug #7616 out of its predicament. It's April 24, 1983, and the combined locomotives are just beginning to move, with #7859 running long hood forward.

(John Lucas)

Here are all four of the Cotton Belt B36-7's together: #7773, 7772, (cabless) 7771, and 7770. At Cabazon, California, on April 24, 1983, the foursome is fighting the worst Beaumont Hill has to offer westbounds—1.9%. Behind the double-stacks on this *AVBAT* is a three-unit midtrain helper, which will be cut out near Colton after assisting this heavy train downhill.

(Bruce Veary)

The odyssey of #7771 has been followed closely in these pages since it was constructed as a prototype B36-7 with a cab in 1980. After a collision, it was slowly rebuilt at Los Angeles with new parts from the builder, who was at the time in the process of introducing a production-model cabless version of its B23/30/36 units. Except for minor details, homemade #7771 compares quite closely with Burlington Northern B30-7's #4000-4052. It is SP's only B-unit at present, and is assigned for maintenance to Pine Bluff, but was photographed at City of Industry in California in June of 1984. *(Bob Gottier)*

Pine Bluff tried some experimental "super gloss" paint on a few units in 1983; the result was a grey so dark and glossy it looked almost blue. It apparently cannot pass the Southern California air pollution tests, so this formulation won't be applied outdoors at Taylor Yard. With a Roman "SP" on the nose, B30-7 #7811 poses at Englewood Yard in Houston in June of 1983. It was built in March, 1978, as part of an order for twenty, #7804-7823. *(Joseph A. Strapac)*

Monster locomotive consists were once unthinkable, but trying times and difficult operations demand the utmost, even from second-generation power. The infamous Searles Shoofly had a ruling grade of 3.67% and tight curves which favored four-axle locomotives—and some of the heaviest trains on the system. Westbound on February 27, 1982 are #7833, 7785, 7793, 7792, 7777, 7848, 8356, and 9237, barely crawling despite a full dose of run-eight on all throttles. *(Tom Taylor)*

Espee's Shasta Line isn't usually thought of as a locale to see grain trains, but here is one at Crescent Lake in February of 1982, waiting to insert a set of midtrain helpers (borrowed from a westbound) for their dynamic braking on the downhill side. Two SD45's and a pair of tunnel motors are led by SD40T-2 #8490, built in January of 1978. It is expected to become #5826 on the SP&SF. *(Ed Collar, Jr.)*

We're at an elevation of 134 feet at Colorado, California, where the SP crosses the Colorado River and enters Arizona. A short run on double track ends just out of sight, as extra 8237 east slows for the bridge. Not far from here is where the river went wild in 1905-07, spilling over into what was then the Salton Sink and creating today's Salton Sea. *(John Totten)*

On page 120, we illustrate the *AVLAT* delivering containers from Avondale (New Orleans) to Los Angeles. The other side of the coin is the *LAAVT*, pictured at Gary, New Mexico on April 24, 1983. With double-stacks at the front, extra 8308 east climbs a hill of .8% before dropping down the last eight miles into Lordsburg and changing crews. "Snoot" SD40T-2 #8308 is from the second series of Locotrol units, #8307-8321, delivered early in 1978. It will carry an even number in the 5740-5820 series on the SP&SF roster.

(John Lucas)

One of those seventy SD40-2 units illustrated in cocoon storage at Eugene in our 1980 Review is pictured at Cable, on Tehachapi, March 20, 1982. The 8200 series was delivered during the 1980 recession and was almost immediately consigned to storage. Unlike the 8300-series Locotrol units, these and the 8500's have short noses since they carry no radio gear. *(Bruce Veary)*

SD40T-2 #8521 leads #6652, 6554, and 6589 on the MBSMF *(Memphis Blue Streak Merchandise)* through Seger, Texas on December 8, 1979. The train is running eastbound by timetable here; its lead unit is part of an order for 75 delivered in 1978-79, #8499-8573, which is currently scheduled to become SP&SF #5825-5909. The GP35's face an uncertain future, with #6554 on its way to scrap as this is written.

(Stuart Schroeder)

Above, freshly-painted SD45 #8898 stops briefly on the westbound mainline at Loma Linda, California, where Beaumont Hill helpers are routinely cut out. The date is March, 1982; #8898 has not yet been scheduled for upgrading at Sacramento. *(Joe Shine)* Below, Cotton Belt #8969 and two compatriots struggle with the westbound *Steel Train* at Eder, a few miles west of the summit at Norden—but almost four hundred feet uphill from here. This unit is scheduled for GRIP treatment in 1986, and will probably emerge with a 6700- series SP&SF number.

(Clint Nestell)

Most of the justly-famed Gaviota Trestle northwest of Santa Barbara gets into the picture as the *Oakland-Los Angeles Trailers*, then running as second #830, glides southward on February 8, 1980 with SD45 #9114 and SD45T-2's #9215 and 9283 on the point. Today, the line from Los Angeles to San Luis Obispo is dispatched via Direct Traffic Control, and train numbers are just a memory. *(John Lucas)*

Espee subsidiary St. Louis Southwestern (the Cotton Belt) pays just a small percentage of its income on debt service, due to a bankruptcy that wiped out its old bonds. As a result, it can spend relatively more on locomotives than its parent, even to the point of providing permanent additions to SP's fleet. Cotton Belt SD45T-2 #9376 leads #9147 and 8488 into a tunnel on the Siskiyou Line in Oregon in 1979. *(Brian T. Thompson)*

The relatively-gentle westbound approach to the Sierra is just .5% at Boca, 26 miles west of Reno, although it will be more demanding as the summit is approached. Four units on the point and two mid-train helpers shatter the calm at Boca on October 6, 1979 with 124 empty Pacific Fruit Express reefers. Cotton Belt SD45T-2 #9396, one of the final series of 20-cylinder machines, is in the lead. It was built in June of 1975.

(Clint Nestell)

Those who wish to accuse this photographer of carrying a portable, "threatening sky" in his camera bag are invited to form a line at the right! Regardless, it was a moody Sunday morning in November of 1977 east of Golconda, Nevada as extra 9326 east racked up the ton-miles behind an SD45T-2 and SD40 #8434 (which has long since become #7306). At this point, the Espee train is on Western Pacific's side of the paired track.

(Ted Benson)

The very last-delivered of the SD45T-2's was captured on film in September of 1978, in a scene impossible to duplicate today. This is a Baltimore & Ohio freight crossing the Kentucky & Indiana Terminal bridge between New Albany, Indiana, and Louisville, Kentucky. Since the CSX merger, B&O trains operate via the more direct SBD route (ex-L&N!) via Worthville, Kentucky...furthermore, the K&IT itself is now part of the Norfolk Southern. *(Dave Arthur)*

Typical of the SD45T-2's bought only by the Southern Pacific and Cotton Belt, #9271 poses at its home port of Roseville on April 10, 1979. Despite its corporate identity, this and other SSW "mountain maulers" are generally held by Southern Pacific in California. The #9271 was built in February of 1973 as part of class EF636C-7, #9261-9281. *(Gordon Lloyd, Jr.)*

Eastbound Cotton Belt #9402 pops out of the night on January 30, 1984 at Niles Tower, orders on the stand giving clearance through Warm Springs on the run east to Watsonville Junction. A new "tower" building planned for 1985 construction will be equally efficient, but hardly so atmospheric. *(Ted Benson)*